NORMAN

About the Author

Stephen Lancaster (Lonaconing, Maryland) has been involved in paranormal research since 1997, conducting investigative work for politicians, military facilities, the board of education, museums, commercial locations, businesses, television, and civilian properties. His research is recognized by the US government. In 2007 he began producing *MonsterVisionTV*, an independent paranormal investigation program with nearly two million views worldwide. Stephen often gives public lectures on paranormal phenomenon and research. His 2017 documentary, *FANTÔME: The Haunting of Brentwood Wine Bistro* was released on October 13, 2017, and the paranormal film shot to #1 in documentaries on the world's largest movie website, IMDb. Visit him online at www.monstervisiontv.net and stay up to date at twitter.com/wraithwrite.

To Write to the Author

If you wish to contact the author or would like more information about this book, please write to the author in care of Llewellyn Worldwide, and we will forward your request. Llewellyn Worldwide cannot guarantee that every letter written to the author can be answered, but all will be forwarded. Please write to:

Stephen Lancaster
℅ Llewellyn Worldwide
2143 Wooddale Drive
Woodbury, MN 55125-2989

Please enclose a self-addressed stamped envelope for reply, or $1.00 to cover costs. If outside the USA, enclose an international postal reply coupon.

STEPHEN LANCASTER

The Doll
That Needed
to Be Locked Away

A TRUE STORY

Llewellyn Worldwide
Woodbury, Minnesota

Norman: The Doll That Needed to Be Locked Away © 2018 by Stephen Lancaster. All rights reserved. No part of this book may be used or reproduced in any manner whatsoever, including Internet usage, without written permission from Llewellyn Publications, except in the case of brief quotations embodied in critical articles and reviews.

First Edition
First Printing, 2018

Book design by Bob Gaul
Cover design by Shira Atakpu
Interior photos provided by Stephen Lancaster

Llewellyn Publications is a registered trademark of Llewellyn Worldwide Ltd.

Library of Congress Cataloging-in-Publication Data (Pending)
ISBN: 978-0-7387-5551-9

Llewellyn Worldwide Ltd. does not participate in, endorse, or have any authority or responsibility concerning private business transactions between our authors and the public.

All mail addressed to the author is forwarded, but the publisher cannot, unless specifically instructed by the author, give out an address or phone number.

Any Internet references contained in this work are current at publication time, but the publisher cannot guarantee that a specific location will continue to be maintained. Please refer to the publisher's website for links to authors' websites and other sources.

Llewellyn Publications
A Division of Llewellyn Worldwide Ltd.
2143 Wooddale Drive
Woodbury, MN 55125-2989
www.llewellyn.com

Printed in the United States of America

Contents

Disclaimer ix

Dedication xi

Acknowledgments xiii

Foreword xv

Introduction 1

  1: The Serpent Beneath It 9

  2: A Mother's Gift 19

  3: Infestation 37

4: The Visitors   49

5: Take the Hint   59

6: Duality   77

7: The Children Speak   83

8: 911   99

9: He Killed   109

10: Haunted Doll for Sale   123

11: I Know   129

12: Hurricane Matthew   141

13: December Chills   165

14: Heart Still Beating   175

15: Christmas Eve 2016   185

16: Ashes   199

17: Rest   205

Afterword   213

Epilogue   219

Disclaimer

I have tried to recreate events, locales, and conversations from my memories of them. In order to maintain their anonymity in some instances, I have changed the names of individuals and places, and I may have changed some identifying characteristics and details, such as physical properties, occupations, and places of residence, to protect the original family and the tragedy they experienced, and one in which we shared.

Dedication

This book is dedicated to my wife, best friend, and research partner, Christina, my parents, Sharon and Stephen, my daughter Lucidity, my stepdaughter Hannah, my grandson Tanner, my dog Tank, and to all of my dear friends.

And, to a girl I never knew.

Acknowledgments

A very special thank you to Rosemary Ellen Guiley, Darren Evans, Amy Glaser, Matt and Tara, Liam and Lyndsay, Cody and Kelia, and A. J. Parker.

Foreword

Dolls are one of the most likely objects to become haunted.

Dolls that have human forms are ideal vessels for residual energy and spirits. Owners, whether adult or child, often form strong emotional bonds to dolls—they become human substitutes.

If something tragic happens to the owner, or if the owner suffers intense unhappy and negative feelings, the bad energy can be transferred to the doll. This energy is residual, but if it is strong enough, it can take on a thought-form presence as a "bad" personality of the doll.

Residual energy can be dormant for long periods of time, but if the doll goes to a new home and owner, and the place and person have the right energy, the residual personality can become activated and cause phenomena in the new house.

There are other ways that dolls can become haunted. Spirits can be attracted to dolls and take up residence in them. They may be attracted by the doll's owner, by the residual energy lodged in the doll, or other unknown factors. Spirits can range from low-level tricksters to more hostile and powerful entities.

They, too, can be dormant until activated by the right circumstances.

In some cases, the spirit might be the earthbound soul of a person, someone who has not made a full transition to the afterlife. An example is a doll owner who dies suddenly and tragically and for various reasons does not cross over because they were lost, confused, or hanging on to unfinished business.

Dolls can also become haunted if they are deliberately used in spirit summoning and spellcasting work. In such cases, spirits are invited to inhabit the dolls.

Removing the doll from the premises alleviates the haunting phenomena in the house in most cases. Sometimes binding spells must be performed on dolls to keep pesky spirits from getting loose and causing havoc.

Earthbound souls need to be helped to the afterlife. If a doll becomes attached due to a spirit attachment to a person, then that becomes an entirely different issue that must be addressed accordingly.

—Rosemary Ellen Guiley

Rosemary Ellen Guiley is one of the leading experts in the paranormal, with more than sixty-five books to her credit.

With John Zaffis, she has coauthored two books on haunted objects: *Haunted by the Things You Love* (2014) and *Demon Haunted: True Stories from the John Zaffis Vault* (2016).

Introduction

It was Christmas Eve of 1968. Festive lights flickered and danced over a blanket of snow throughout the neighborhood, where people were rejoicing, singing, and enjoying laughs and the company of friends and family.

There stood a six-year-old girl outside of her home watching it burn to the ground. She stood barefoot in the snow and in her nightgown, unable to blink or look away from the fire.

From her right hand dangled her doll Matty.

According to first responders who arrived on the scene, the young girl seemed dead to the outside elements as she stood in bitter snow up to her ankles.

Her mother and dog died in the fire. Her brother had died before he was even born. He would have been her twin.

She was taken away and placed in various foster homes until she became an adult. All she ever had of her family were lucid memories and that doll.

Not much was said about the incident.

The cause of the fire was never determined and this little girl lost her entire family. Before birth and after birth, death had become this child.

However, there was a secret. A secret only she knew.

That secret would be whispered in my ear forty-eight years later.

Typically I chronicle multiple paranormal cases in my literary work, but this story is one of its own. It deserves to be its own.

So let's start with the introduction and let the rest be the nightmare that it is.

I think it is safe to say my life is still firmly planted in the world of the supernatural and unexplained. But it was not supposed to be like this.

My life has been one unbelievable event after the next. Just when I get comfortable and think that I have seen and done it all, another wave of charming irresistibility comes crashing in, sending me into the deep waters of unpredictability.

Sometimes the water of those eventful oceans I am drowning in is so cloudy that it is hard to determine which way to swim to find the surface. Sometimes I swim deeper and sometimes I find a breath. However, many times the sea of curiosity I so frequently float in takes me to places that become unimaginable mental and physical scars.

My name is Stephen Lancaster. I am a published author specializing in paranormal phenomena. My stories chronicle the past twenty years of heavy and nearly obsessive work in the field of paranormal research.

I have researched hundreds of supernatural cases since 1997. Those cases ranged from traditional residential and commercial hauntings, alleged demonic possessions, UFOs and extraterrestrial sightings, to cryptozoological work. I have also handled extreme cases in military facilities, and I've done the same for politicians.

I guess you could say I have been more than knee-deep in a bizarre, very blessed, and curious world. This is my life and what I am about to share with you is no different.

I was hoping it would be much different at this point. But things change, or in this case, they don't.

I retired from the field in November 2013. During the summer of 2016 I found myself once again being challenged with the unbelievable task of finding the truth to supernatural mysteries. Once again I found myself raising the tolerance on the bar of belief.

You know, it is a tick that refuses to go away. It is an unbeatable magnetic force that draws me back time and time again.

I tried to retire from the field of paranormal research. After nearly two decades of work, I felt it was time. I tried to walk away and I tried to leave that world behind.

However, that tick of curiosity never stopped. It just kept pounding in my head until I finally realized my purpose.

I had to come to terms with who I was and, more importantly, who I am. I could not lie to myself anymore.

I stared into the mirror every day for the past year and a half, attempting to talk myself out of what would become the inevitable. I would stare and say, "Don't do it Lancaster. Don't do it."

But I was only fooling myself.

Paranormal research has been such a huge part of my life. The field was and is my passion.

When my world went dark and dismal years ago and the dead started entering and affecting my life, I thought the best thing at the time was to turn the other cheek. I thought the best thing for me was to leave the terror of the dark spirits behind. I thought the best thing to do was move on to the stereotypical modern and—dare I say—normal American life.

I wanted to start a new life. I wanted to start a life not so dead.

Of course you can probably figure out that my retirement was cut short and I had to dust off the equipment cases, pull my moth-eaten clothes out of an old trunk, and hook that rabbit's foot back onto my vest.

Most of the equipment I used in the field had long been sold, destroyed, or given away to fellow researchers and investigators. So I was starting from scratch, just like I did back in 1997.

Back then I was armed with very little. I started with a compass, a few flashlights, a rabbit's foot, a notepad, and not much else. This was a very familiar feeling.

But how and why I came out of retirement is how this story begins.

If not for walking into an antique shop at just the right time, my house and my life would be completely normal. But instead I left the shop that day and willingly welcomed into my home something I could never possibly ignore.

This led to credit card swipe after credit card swipe after credit card swipe. I found myself rebuilding all of my research equipment. My family needed it.

It's kind of difficult to leave the paranormal world behind, especially when that world is the heart of you.

I could no longer sit back and forget about the ghosts, the hauntings, the monsters, or the people I helped along the way.

I could no longer ignore it.

It isn't easy to just turn the other cheek when your own home becomes the target of something evil. It isn't easy when the occurrences defy all rational and logical thought.

I brought something into my home that I never under any circumstance felt would be dangerous.

But *he* is.

So I began doing what I do best—watching the dead.

This was new territory for me. I spent the past twenty years studying and researching paranormal events, but I never gave enough of my time to the possibility of objects being haunted or becoming possessed with a malevolent entity. The idea was novel to me and nothing more.

I certainly was open to the possibility, but to be honest, my services were never requested to explore such phenomena. People sought out my expertise for traditional paranormal exploration, such as researching to prove or disprove deceased loved ones haunting their homes.

Ironically, I have quite the collection of allegedly haunted objects. I guess you can't immerse yourself in the field of paranormal research for so long without picking up a few hitchhikers along the way.

The majority of objects I've obtained were literally given to me with express orders to take them far away from a relevant property with a promise never to return them.

However, Norman was different. I sought out Norman and made sure he ended up mine. To this day I'm not really sure why I found myself wanting the doll so badly.

Perhaps it was the dismal history attached to the doll, or just the excitement and disbelief of actually stumbling upon the *real* one.

And I strongly emphasize the word *real* in that last sentence.

He is nor man nor toy. He is Norman.

My personal experiences with Norman coupled with half a dozen eyewitness testimonies made me a firm believer in the possibility of objects becoming authentically haunted.

I know for a fact that Norman is possessed. His intent and origin is still up for debate, but considering what I have seen, I believe he won't stop until he gets what he wants.

You have read story after story and seen movie after movie about haunted dolls, but how many of us actually believe that phenomenon to be real?

I never thought the day would come when I would actually acknowledge a toy being possessed. But, considering everything I have seen over the past twenty years, I shouldn't be that surprised.

The sleepless nights, the night terrors, and an endless amount of nightmares. I can't even begin to count how many nights I awoke screaming at the thought of a knife to my neck.

The following is my personal account with the haunted doll.

1

The Serpent Beneath It

"Look like the innocent flower, but be the serpent under it."

William Shakespeare said that.

I couldn't find a more fitting quote to sum up the intentions of a would-be monster locked away inside a child's toy.

But what are haunted dolls? You have heard the countless stories and you have seen the endless movies. But what really are they?

To put it simply, they are often vessels for malevolent spirits to manipulate the human environment: a Trojan horse if you will.

Psychopath in an innocent package with a dash of sociopath is how I tend to describe a haunted doll.

This phenomenon is nothing new, however. In fact, stories of haunted or possessed dolls date back to ancient Egypt, where they were actually constructed intentionally.

That's right. They were actually built to be evil.

Most of the time they were used during war in the same fashion the more commonly known voodoo doll is used.

If they wanted somebody dead, like Ramses III, for instance, they made dolls that shared his likeness with the purpose of causing his death.

In theory, whatever harm you bring to the doll in turn occurs to the individual it represents.

Throughout history, African, Native American, and European cultures have used dolls for mystical purposes. Although in many cases they were used for religious rituals, they were more commonly used to bind evil spirits.

The idea was to trap the unwanted "ghost" in something that could easily be buried, burned, or removed from an area altogether.

As history has taught us, binding evil spirits voluntarily or involuntarily to dolls often brought forth a not so pleasant ending.

When have you ever heard of a happy-go-lucky haunted doll?

Since the beginning, something unfathomable has always been attached to the use of them.

Haunted objects are a staple to the field of paranormal research. The energy of a spirit, for one reason or another, can and will attach itself to anything of its choosing.

It could simply be because of admiration for a particular object or because the spirit simply can't let go of that favorite teddy bear or rocking chair.

In those cases, the spiritual energy is benign.

But when it wants to be able to move, and when there is sinister intent involved, the spirit needs an inanimate object that can be animated.

Rosemary's opening statement in her foreword raises many questions. She says, "Dolls are one of the most likely objects to become haunted."

But why?

Dolls are the ultimate masquerade.

They are pretty, smiling, crying, talking replicas of babies and people in general. They walk, crawl, blink, and mechanically do anything a human being can. Some even wet themselves.

They are designed to be brought to life by a child's imagination. We as human beings are the masters of puppets. However, in rare cases they are brought to life by something else. Dolls are innocent, and they are the last thing anybody would ever view as evil without interior manipulation.

Like the toy gun looking and sounding the part but bringing no harm, there are real ones. They are controlled by a hand with either good or bad intentions behind it. Nature breeds life and nature takes it away. Man builds things, and life comes back. But that life returns from a place we have yet to even begin to understand.

Many haunted dolls and the stories attached to them have become household names throughout the years. Their history and existence have been immortalized through literature and film.

Hollywood wasted no time capitalizing on this phenomenon to scare the pants off the horror movie aficionado.

Unfortunately, the glamorized exposure has placed the thought of possessed dolls in the realm of fiction. But in reality it is nothing to be nonchalant about or dismiss altogether.

It has been my job for decades to uncover the truth and separate the facts from the fabricated in the paranormal field. I assure you, my friends, the truth behind some of these stories does exist.

I watch the movies and I read the books, but for me it is simply for entertainment. *Chucky* cracks me up.

But is *Chucky* a product of Hollywood, or does he have origins rooted in truth?

Fact of the matter is, *Chucky* is loosely based on the stories of Robert the Doll.

Robert the Doll was acquired by author Robert Eugene Otto in 1906. It was given to him by a voodoo practicing Bahamian servant at that time.

Otto's neighbors often reported seeing the doll move from window to window in his house.

His parents also claimed the doll would speak. While young Otto was playing and talking to the doll, his parents often heard a second speaker in a completely different voice responding to their child.

In many cases the voices overlapped, proving the young Otto wasn't simply making Robert "pretend" talk in an altered voice.

The experiences with Robert still occur to this day. He currently resides at the East Martello Museum in Key West, Florida, where strange activity is often reported.

Robert found his mainstream fame in the 1988 horror film *Child's Play*, as well as related sequels as a character named Chucky.

However, Robert isn't the only one.

Thanks to the popular horror films *The Conjuring*, *Annabelle*, *The Conjuring 2*, and *Annabelle: Creation*, you have most likely heard of Annabelle.

Like Robert, Annabelle has her true story, and it is far from the on-screen adaptations.

This may surprise you, but she isn't as horrific in appearance as the movies want you to believe.

In fact, Annabelle was nothing more than the infamous Raggedy Ann doll that was first created in 1915.

Annabelle's real appearance.

Raggedy Ann saw many alterations and variations in her design throughout the years.

In 1970, a student nurse was given a more up-to-date version of the doll.

Shortly after receiving the gift, she and her roommate started to experience strange behavior from the doll.

She then contacted a psychic medium who deemed the toy haunted and possessed by the spirit of a young girl named Annabelle Higgins. The girl allegedly died on the property the doll originated from.

After considering what the medium told her, the nurse insisted on attempting to live with the possessed doll.

Eventually the activity began to escalate well beyond her comfort zone. Claims surfaced that the doll had the ability to bleed and the dexterity to write messages. The two roommates were shaken up.

The nurse sought out paranormal investigators Ed and Lorraine Warren for further assistance.

Ed concluded from his research that Annabelle was demonically possessed, and the Warrens convinced the doll's owner to allow them to take it, and they did.

The Warrens have received an onslaught of scrutiny over the years. Many people are skeptical of their methods and claims, considering the majority of their stories only have Ed's word to go by with nothing else to reference.

This includes Annabelle. There is nothing in print or historically documented to support the claims concerning the doll that wasn't written by Ed himself.

Regardless, Annabelle became famous.

Following that, the Warrens profited greatly on Annabelle through literary work, lectures, and, of course, films.

Annabelle currently resides under lock and key at the Warrens' Occult Museum in Monroe, Connecticut.

But what about the stories you don't hear? What about the stories that haven't been capitalized upon?

I think dolls are center stage due to their realistic features that cause the brain to relate human function to supernatural function.

They already look alive to begin with.

I have been collecting haunted objects for years. The items I have acquired range from dolls, to stuffed animals, to musical boxes, to bones, to even clothes and Ouija boards.

With the exception of Norman, I have never purchased a haunted item; they were always given to me. And even considering Norman, I did not know he was haunted at the time.

In cases where my clients felt it was a certain object leading to their haunting, they would often give it to me just to be rid of it.

Whether it would be my research proving it, or the owner's own belief, many locations have gotten rid of their spiritual problems after simply handing off the object to me.

That's how living your research becomes a blessing and a curse. I collect the objects for multiple reasons.

For starters, it helps my clients once again find peace and comfort in their home or business.

Secondly, it gives me the opportunity to research at will.

My collection consists of items from all over the world, all with a different story attached...and in some cases, something else.

When things at your house start to go bump in the night, it proves to be rather difficult to determine the origin when your home is already full of other people's ghosts.

However, in most cases, the spiritual activity attached to what we brought into our home was and still is harmless.

It is nothing for us to hear a voice or find something out of place or witness a door opening and closing. We've become used to it. I guess you can't expect to live the life we do as researchers and at the same time have the privilege of turning it off at will.

It must be accepted going into it. Your life will never be the same.

So with that, we take chances.

A few years ago, there was a stone that Christina collected from a case we were working on for the Mayor. That stone would appear at random, all through the house. We would find it in our cars, in the bathroom, on a shelf, or on the floor. Nothing evil ever derived from it, but this happened so many times it could not be ignored.

Another case involved a talking stuffed animal that somehow had the ability to curse at you. It was designed to speak, but only speak a certain number of pleasant phrases. But this thing just randomly cursed at you when you walked by. There was one night in particular when Christina woke me up claiming the toy had said my name at least three times.

All of those experiences were simple and passive. There was never a worry about an evil entity being attached.

We are blessed with the luxury of home field research.

I can't even begin to say there is a way to remove a spirit from a certain place or from a particular object. I stop my involvement at observe and report.

I can say having removed items myself that the haunting ceased at each given location, but the spirit still remained in its vessel. The only difference was that vessel was now in my possession.

Today is very different for the field of paranormal research. We have equipment and knowledge that wasn't available fifty years ago.

Now haunted dolls or allegedly haunted items can truly be studied. We can conduct tests to either validate or disprove what was once believed to be paranormal in origin; it's no longer about choosing whether or not to believe a person's story.

And now I had that incredible opportunity.

However, before we jump right into the home surveillance, my personal research, the physical encounters, the voices, the attacks, and the infestations, I need to start this retelling at the day we visited an antique shop located on the outskirts of Wallace, North Carolina.

That was the day we welcomed a new boy to the family.

2

A Mother's Gift

It was the peak of the summer, and as expected, the Southern heat suffocated you with every breath. Typically one welcomed this with sweet iced tea and a powerful fan, but this particular summer welcomed something else.

And then this particular summer welcomed a winter colder than any other I could dare compare it to.

My girlfriend and I were browsing around the old antique shop looking for anything of interest.

I was at the back of the store when my eyes made contact with a rough looking wooden box sitting in a high chair on top of a tall wooden shelf. In fact, it was so high the box nearly touched the ceiling, and my arms could barely manage to grab the bottom legs of the high chair.

This box was not for sale. There was no price tag. We are both suckers for unique looking boxes.

I quickly found Christina so she could help me balance the high chair holding the box while I brought it to the floor.

This box was wicked to say the least.

The symbol instantly reminded me of the fleur-de-lis and my time as a scout during my much younger days. But the fleur-de-lis is rooted in legend itself.

It is believed the symbol, sharing the same characteristics as the lotus flower, represented perfection, light, and…life.

The lock for the box had been removed in an attempt to keep anybody from opening it.

Well, at least that is my best guess.

Please excuse the image quality of the box. All I had on me to take pictures with was a cheap cell phone.

The most peculiar part of the box was what appeared to be scratch marks.

Four scratch marks either trying to get in or desperately trying to get out.

But again, that is all speculation.

We glanced around the antique shop to see if anybody was looking.

I pulled out a pocket knife, stuck it in the hole at an angle where the lock used to be, and pulled the door open.

Upon opening the box, we discovered a doll and a God-awful odor. The smell of time and history.

Doll box missing lock.

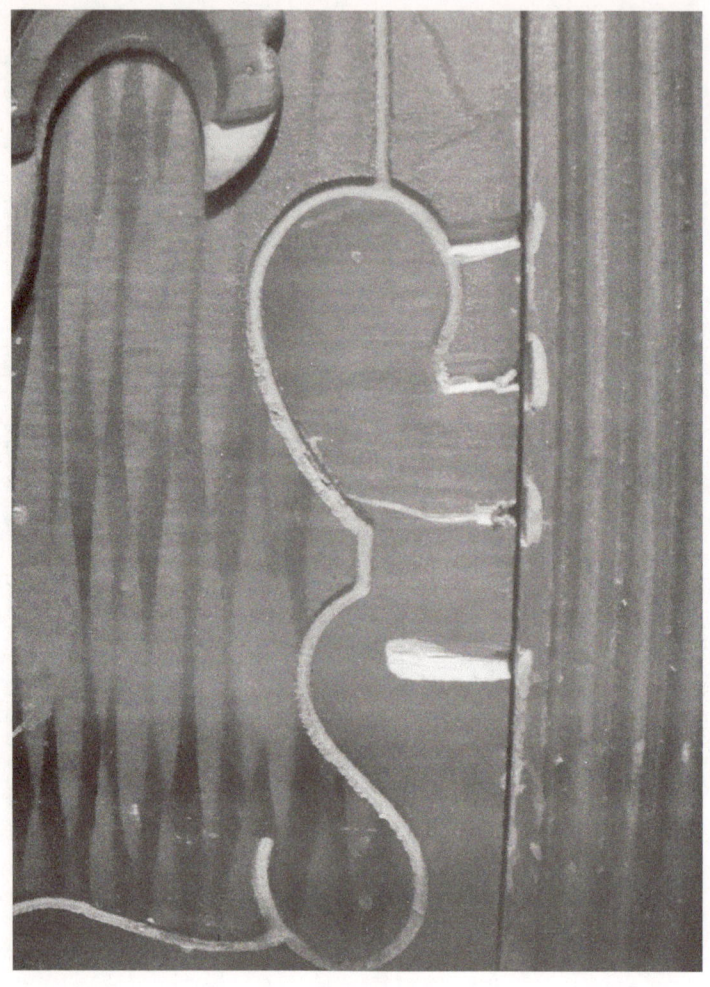
Claw marks on the box.

Upon a closer look, we revealed his origin. The doll, named Matty Mattel, was originally created by the toy manufacturing company Mattel in 1961.

A quick search on my phone revealed all there was to know about our new discovery.

Before his physical creation, Matty acted as the boy mascot for the company.

From 1955 to 1970 he played a huge role in the marketing for the toy company. He even returned again in the 1980s.

In the 1960s, Matty was famous. He hosted television's Sunday morning cartoon *Matty's Funday Funnies* between 1961 and 1963.

Ironically, or coincidentally, depending on how you look at it, *Casper the Friendly Ghost* was a big part of *Matty's Funday Funnies*.

After the introduction of their first talking doll, Chatty Cathy, in 1960, Mattel began producing talking versions of Matty and Casper the following year. Matty acted as the company's official logo from 1959 until 1970. I doubt Mattel ever thought one of their creations would become a walking, talking shell harboring our soon-to-be hell.

But how in the world did he end up on the top shelf of an old antique shop?

At that point it didn't matter. He was an antique and we wanted him.

Photo I took of Matty.

I was mesmerized by his look. Like me, Christina was also captivated by his sly demeanor and weathered age.

This doll had a set of eyes, and I know you know the kind I am talking about. Those eyes that seem to follow your every movement no matter which direction you move.

He had a sinister little grin like that of a little boy knowing he just got away with doing something he should not have or that look of patiently waiting for a staged prank to go off.

Our research also indicated that the doll was not manufactured and distributed in the box we were holding.

So, he was stored differently by somebody else. And whoever it was made sure it wasn't going to be easy to open it.

After getting him safely into our hands, I placed the high chair back up where it came from.

That's when I noticed the entire back of the box had something written on it.

I quickly took a few pictures with my cell phone once again. In hindsight, I am glad I did.

On the back interior of the box was a poem, but this was no ordinary poem.

Some of the words were carved, while others appeared to have been written in pencil.

But one thing both Tina and I agreed on was it didn't appear to have been written all at the same time. The style of handwriting changed with what seemed to be each passage.

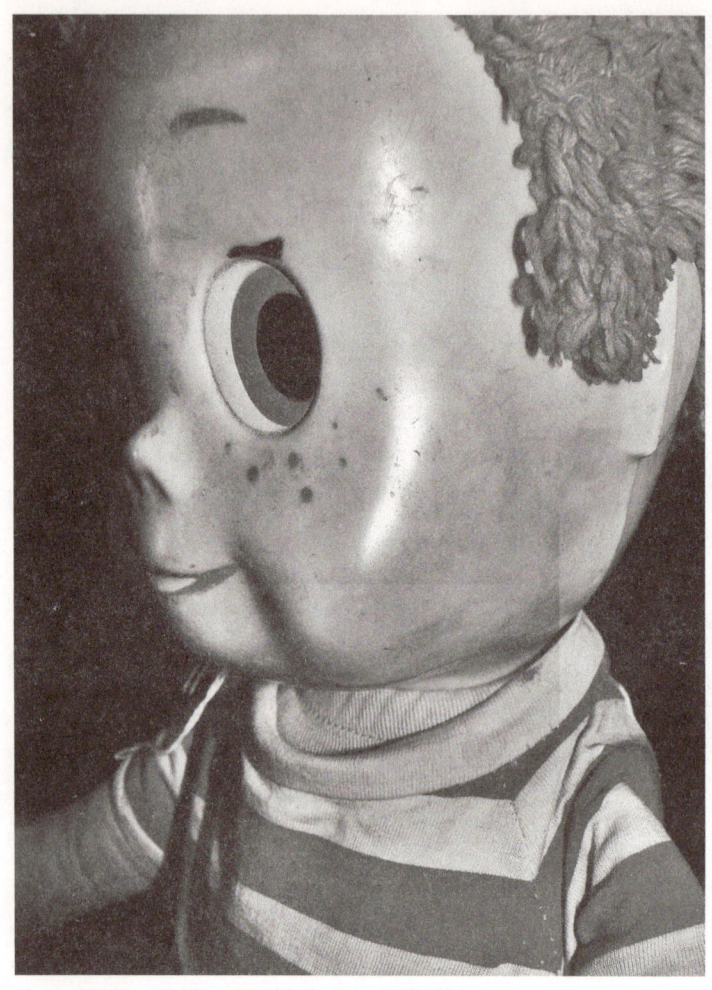

Another photo I took of Matty.

Carving and writing inside the box.

I did my best to make out what the entire thing said at a later time based on the photographs and some video I shot with my cell phone. Some of it was very difficult to read, but in the end I figured it all out.

> *The twelve inch snow glistened under the cold, blank winter sky as the raging fire engulfed her home with a twinkle in her eye.*
>
> *The snow appeared orange like light from a dream as the trees began crying from the death they had seen.*

More carving and writing inside the box.

    A girl stood shivering as she looked into the blaze and the six-year-old would never be the same.
    Ashes rained down upon her like newly fallen snow. There she stood shivering with her arms dangling low.
    Her face remained frozen for a while, holding only the hand of her best friend; a doll with a menacing smile.
    A child's Christmas never came for only death was delivered on the eve of that day.
    Her mother and her dog burned to the ground in the midnight fog.

> *The sound of sirens and whistles filled the smoke glazed air as the little girl stood with a cold, blank stare.*
>
> *No words would ever cross her bitter lips again for the night before Christmas smiled with a sinister grin.*
>
> *So the story was told about an evil occurring when the lights went out and a creature was stirring.*

This was definitely not something I would be reading to the grandchildren around the holidays. It was obvious that it was not written by a child. Not unless she was a six-year-old prodigy. As if that wasn't haunting enough, the poem was validated by the clerks of the shop in the moments ahead.

Our attention went back to the doll.

We both noticed that the doll was not labeled for sale. He just appeared to be put up and out of the way to add to the already antique flair the store encompassed.

But I wanted him, and I was going to charm my way through the nice elderly ladies at the front counter to get him.

Christina and I made our way to the checkout counter, and we were pleasantly greeted by the two women who ran the store.

I immediately asked one of the ladies how much the doll cost. With deadpan faces, they quickly looked at one another without saying a word.

After a weird moment of silence, the one lady said the doll wasn't for sale and insinuated in a very cryptic fashion that I would not want the doll anyway.

I played dumb and pulled out some reverse psychology. I basically said she was right and the doll was all dirty anyway, so it probably wasn't worth anything.

But I couldn't help but ask as to why the doll wasn't for sale. I was assuming a childhood attachment, or that maybe the doll had sentimental value to somebody at the store, but I was wrong.

The lady behind the counter proceeded to tell us that the doll came from a very sad home and that whatever sadness was in the home came with him.

So I immediately asked if they believed there was some sort of spiritual attachment.

The other lady spoke up, questioning my interest in the doll.

So now the stage was set...

...I told the women who I was and what I had spent my life doing. Christina is professionally a nurse, but over the past seven years or so has become a paranormal investigator and has accompanied me during field work.

They were both intrigued, and that initial barrier disappeared in both of them and they let their guard down.

It was almost as if they were relieved to meet somebody so interested in spiritual phenomena.

They proceeded to give this author a story.

The ladies told us the doll had come from a woman who lost a child during birth. She was pregnant with twins—one boy and one girl.

In July 1962, Matty the doll was given as a gift to the expecting mother at the hospital from an unknown source. During the moments of childbirth, she tragically lost one of the twins due to medical complications.

Shortly after, she arrived home with her new daughter and "Matty."

It was from that point, for whatever reasons and for whatever took place inside that house, the woman believed her dead son to be inside of Matty.

As they continued with the story, I could only imagine the heartache and psychological damage that the lady must have endured.

I was curious, however. Here we had a potentially haunted doll with the spirit of an unborn child. My mind was racing.

How does that work? If real, how does that work? I just kept repeating that to myself.

I mean, does the spirit grow inside the doll alongside his sister? I would certainly subscribe to the idea that a spirit could learn based on repeated observation.

It is scientific fact our bodies are of bioelectrical makeup. We have electricity in our bodies. When we die, that electricity or that energy goes somewhere. Energy is infinite and it does not die. It simply changes form.

So what's to say the energy from that unborn baby wasn't transferred into the-then "Matty?"

It seems believable to think that a spirit could watch and learn and become educated just as a child would over years and years of living with a family.

I don't know how far this went behind closed doors with the bereaving mother. I don't know what really happened. I have a yarn from two old ladies.

There was a fire that ultimately killed the mother. We do know that. We do know the daughter survived with Matty in hand.

According to the clerks at the shop, the fifty-year-old doll was brought into the store by the daughter in 2014.

It is interesting to think that the surviving twin had kept the doll for fifty-four years, since it came into the house in 1962. She grew up with it and kept it close well into her adulthood.

I guess she viewed Matty as the brother she was supposed to have but never did.

By that logic, we were looking at a fifty-four-year-old male soul attached to a doll.

That was a very interesting, yet depressing, story of the doll's history, but at the moment it didn't really mean anything.

At this point, one of the ladies looked at me and said, "How about five dollars?"

Both Christina and I, with almost too much enthusiasm, answered back, "We'll take it!"

Looking back, I wish I would have realized the responsibility and risk of accepting such an offer.

When Matty was handed to me, I made a comment suggesting that he looked like hell.

The woman who sold me Matty replied by saying I was half right. She said that something coming from hell was bound to look like it.

I attempted to lighten the mood by digging up that classic phrase—you can't judge a book by its cover.

Even then, the mood remained the same as she snapped back intently. She leaned over the counter toward my face and put her hand on the doll. She looked at me and said, "This is no book."

I laughed, took a few steps back, and said, "Well, if everything you said is true, it will be one day."

We left the store with our new addition, and I couldn't help but think those two elderly women must have had experiences of their own. But they weren't talking.

There was obviously a reason they believed the doll to be evil. There was obviously a reason the surviving twin gave him up.

At the time, that short and overdramatic conversation during the transaction seemed like nothing more than a funny and trivial story to tell friends.

That notion quickly went away.

There are many elements involved in rationalizing or accepting a paranormal event. First there is shock, then disbelief, then acceptance found in either proving or disproving. This particular chapter in my life was no exception.

As my brain tends to do, I was interweaving what was said and doing mathematical equations in my head, which ultimately led to a coincidence.

We left, in such a hurry to get home that we completely forgot the wooden box. That was the entire reason for us pulling it down in the first place.

I could kick myself now for leaving it. I decided we would just go back and pick it up some other time. I then mentioned to Christina that the doll was originally brought home fifty-four years ago in July, following that lady giving birth. I continued by pointing out that we had found the doll in July and we were now taking it home.

Everything is relative and one event sets in motion the next.

So, there we were.

It wasn't Christmas Eve, but it was perplexing to ponder that a night of giving can easily become a night of taking away.

Maybe Matty felt cheated and jaded and wanted to bequeath the same fate on his family. They expected gifts. He expected the gift of life. His was taken, and so was his mother's.

Did he blame her?
It was all speculation.

3

Infestation

Later that night, we sat in the master bedroom of our home examining Matty. He didn't do much.

His head would move in one direction, side to side. He had a pull string on his back that released a few garbled phrases that were obviously articulated better during his youth.

Now they just sounded like a demon gargling razor blades while reciting some weird Latin phrase.

Matty had everything on the list for a stereotypical-looking haunted doll. I just didn't think he would actually be haunted.

Our dog Tank came into the bedroom and as soon as his eyes lined up with Matty's, he began to cower and walk backward out of the room. Tank did not break eye contact with the doll until he was clear of our bedroom. This I found extremely odd. It's nothing for dogs to become spooked by the simplest of things. But with Tank, the only time I had ever witnessed him doing such a thing was when he was with me during investigations of highly spiritual locations.

So I called Tank back into the room. Again, with hesitation, he refused to come near Matty.

As I write this, four months after we first brought the doll into our home, Tank will still not approach him.

Shortly after experimenting with Tank, I decided to rename the doll from his factory given name of Matty to something that made him ours.

I tossed a handful of names around before settling. I considered Smurf, Plankton, Grumpy, Lonnie, and pretty much any other title I could think of that represented something small, unisex, and benign.

Then it hit me.

Norman. That name was perfect.

I mean he didn't look normal, and we all know Norman Bates from the movie *Psycho* certainly wasn't either. It just seemed fitting and novel.

Hindsight is always 20/20.

That night we placed Norman on the headboard of our bed alongside a row of other allegedly haunted dolls and toys we've acquired over the years.

That was supposed to be the end of it. I saw Norman as a conversation piece at best.

Later that evening Christina's oldest son Matthew stopped by with his wife Tara and their two children. It was just a friendly visit. Of course they asked about Norman.

I found it funny how Matthew described the newly renamed Matty—"creepy as shit." The coincidence tickled me. Matthew's son Liam took a particular liking to Norman, fiddling with his head and pulling the string.

I was sitting at my desk while Christina and Matthew were sitting on the bed when all of a sudden Matthew jumped up from the bed in a panic and literally ran into the bathroom and slammed the door shut.

I'm sure he is going to appreciate me telling that part of the story.

But I was confused at first. I had no idea what could have prompted such a fearful retreat. Within a second Christina jumped up from the bed. It turned out to be a giant spider making its way up the center of the bed.

Now some people are afraid of spiders, and some are not. Turns out the only one of us not afraid was Matthew's wife Tara, who took it upon herself to remove said arachnid.

From discovery to death, the event happened so fast that none of us were able to identify the species. Frankly, I was happy to identify it as dead. My apologies go out to spider enthusiasts.

After the excitement, Matthew and his family left and Christina and I retired for the evening.

At about one in the morning I awoke to something crawling up my leg. Like a deranged monkey on too much caffeine I smacked my leg and killed yet another spider.

By the looks of the remains, it was the same species as the one previously extinguished earlier in the night.

This of course woke Christina, and now becoming completely paranoid about spiders in the bed, we literally sprayed a barrier of bug spray around the bed.

This may all seem like irrelevant nonsense, but this was the first time a spider was ever found in our bed, let alone two of them.

The next morning we searched high and low for a nest or a reason for the spiders to be there. We found nothing.

To my knowledge, most North Carolina spiders avoid people. For now we called this all a coincidence.

That afternoon Christina was lying on the bed reading with me at my desk once again. I glanced over at her and saw yet another spider crawling up the side of the bed toward her.

I jumped up and grabbed her. She had no clue as to why until I had her off the bed and showed her the spider.

I should have called this chapter the great spider massacre of 2016, since we were now up to three.

This prompted us to tear apart the bedroom, pull the bed away, and search once again for the source of those spiders.

Nothing was found.

Next came the rats.

Rats in the kitchen. Rats in the bathroom. Rats in the bedroom.

If there ever was a horror movie checklist, we were quickly progressing through that checklist.

Just like the spiders before them, we never had any issues with anything other than the little common household mouse every now and again. But even that was rare.

I mean we had four dogs inside and half a dozen cats outside. It would be hard-pressed for any little critter to get past that army.

Later that evening Christina screamed at the top of her lungs at the sight of a rat staring back at her in the kitchen. It was sitting right on the kitchen stove.

Then another one darted across the kitchen floor.

Then in the bathroom and then in the closet. One was even in the toilet.

It was total chaos for a moment when they started coming out of the walls in the closet.

I'm not talking swarms like locusts. Don't get me wrong.

One would pop out then disappear, followed by another, or a few at a time.

We regrouped on the bed while discussing a run to the store for rat poison. It was at that moment we could hear faintly from within the walls a band of little squeaks.

Christina said she didn't care if I took down the wall to find them, and that's exactly what I did. Meanwhile, Norman sat on our headboard giving me that sly little grin.

I took down the wall in the closet and in the living room.

I was amazed to see what appeared to be baby rats. It was as if they were just born.

Interestingly enough, we never heard them up until that moment, nor had we ever seen a rat in the house, but in the past twenty-four hours our home had become the wild kingdom.

Resting easy that night wasn't exactly on the radar when every tickle of a hair made you jump thinking it was a spider or a rat.

We sat in the kitchen for a while, completely disgusted at the infestation.

It is unnerving to think about when the grandchildren visited so often.

But nothing prepared either one of us for what happened as we called it a night.

I am thankful to this day that the bedroom light was on when Christina decided to crawl into bed.

I was in the bathroom when I flinched at the sound of her screaming and demanding I come back into the bedroom.

Of course I stopped what I was doing immediately and ran to her aid.

Christina had uncovered a snake that had been waiting underneath our blankets.

This was horrifying.

Destroyed wall in an attempt to find rats.

Now I am not afraid of snakes, but I immediately threw the blankets back over it. You could easily see the serpent starting to move beneath our comforter. What the hell was going on? This was borderline insane.

I waited for the right moment to trap and wrap up the blankets to form a sack.

Following that I immediately ran outside, across our yard, across the road, and into a large field with the confined snake.

With every step I took, I kept saying out loud, "Please don't bite, please don't bite," over and over.

I had no clue what type of snake it was or whether or not it was even venomous. But no chances were being taken regardless.

I threw the blankets down into the grass of the field.

The sun was just starting to vanish thanks to the long days of summer, so I had enough light to see our intruder slither out and make his way through the grass.

I made my way back to the house just in time for Christina to demand I throw the blankets in the washer. Yes, she *demanded*. She wasn't having it, and at least she didn't ask me to burn them.

That night we slept with our eyes open without any blankets and pretty much on top of each other.

It's kind of funny now in a very small way.

In the paranormal world, it is not uncommon for a haunting to invoke such phenomena.

Infestation 45

Rats, spiders, snakes, and other insects often appear in abundance to accompany a haunting.

In past cases, I've witnessed this dozens of times over. But I still wasn't ready to associate Norman with our recent odd experiences. Maybe we just needed a normal exterminator.

The next day we set up an appointment with a local exterminator to give us a quote on removing all of our unwanted guests.

To my surprise, other than finding an irrelevant amount of household spiders and a few other insects here and there, the exterminator insisted our place did not warrant his services.

Flies on our windows.

More flies on windows.

I questioned the guy and told him everything, but he had no explanation for it, other than that God worked in mysterious ways.

He offered to spray for termites and set up some traps. I'm assuming he was trying to make his buck, but I declined. I did appreciate his honesty, however.

Instead, we brought in a cat for interior vermin reconnaissance. We named him Little F.

For respective purposes, you can use your own imagination as to what F stands for. It rhymes with duck if you need a hint.

To be honest, I enjoyed taking him to the vet for shots the first time and hearing the receptionist call for "Little F." She refused to say his full name. She just grinned at me.

Little F and I were inseparable. If only that was the case for him. As it turns out, he was very separable.

4

The Visitors

To this day my stomach still sinks and my anxiety goes through the roof when I hear *knock knock knock* at the front door. I certainly suffer from synesthesia. I hear the knocks and my body chemistry changes. It's similar to when you think of food and your mouth starts to water.

With me, it isn't a pleasant experience. You know what feeling I am talking about. That feeling when you are surprised or startled and your stomach experiences a quick, stabbing sensation. All the while your heart feels as if it just about jumped out of your chest.

Well if it wasn't for constant late-night visitors pounding on our front door, we would never have set up the surveillance system like we did.

And that surveillance system gave us the undeniable proof that Norman was and is alive.

It was early one afternoon and my dogs started barking like they typically do if they see anything or anybody in our yard.

I jumped up from my desk, looked out the windows, and saw nothing. Yet the dogs were as anxious as they could get.

They followed and surrounded me to each window I would peer out.

I figured it was just some neighborhood kids playing pranks on the scary old paranormal guy. But the dogs kept persisting.

Every other day, random knocking at the front door would occur, causing the same chain of events to take place as before.

After about the sixth time over the span of just a few days, I called the police to report harassment.

By the time law enforcement arrived, twenty minutes had passed since the last triple knock, so there wasn't even a slim chance they would find who was doing it without conducting full-on twenty-four-hour surveillance.

About an hour after I wrapped up my report with the police, once again somebody was knocking at my front door and once again the dogs were going nuts.

I ran as fast as I could to the door only to discover nothing upon opening it. At this point I was beyond frustrated. Christina arrived home and I told her about the constant phantom knocking. She too felt uneasy about it.

Later that night, or should I say very early the next morning, we had another visitor. But this time, I was able to catch a glimpse.

The dogs started sounding off once again at four in the morning. I jumped out of bed and looked out the window to see a very sickly looking blonde woman standing on our front porch. I'm guessing here, but she looked to be around forty years old.

She was pounding and pounding on the door, showing signs of dire urgency.

She would knock in sequences of three. *Pound pound pound. Pound pound pound.*

I yelled out the door asking who she was and what she wanted. She said nothing in return.

By the time I was able to get back to the window, she was walking off slowly, disappearing into the darkness of the neighboring woods.

We never saw her again, and still to this day we have no clue whether or not she was the cause of all the previous knocking, related to Norman in some way, or just at the wrong place at the wrong time.

She remains a mystery.

It was at that moment that Christina and I jumped on the computer and ordered a new surveillance system for the house. We even went ahead and ordered just about everything imaginable for use in paranormal research considering the recent events at the house.

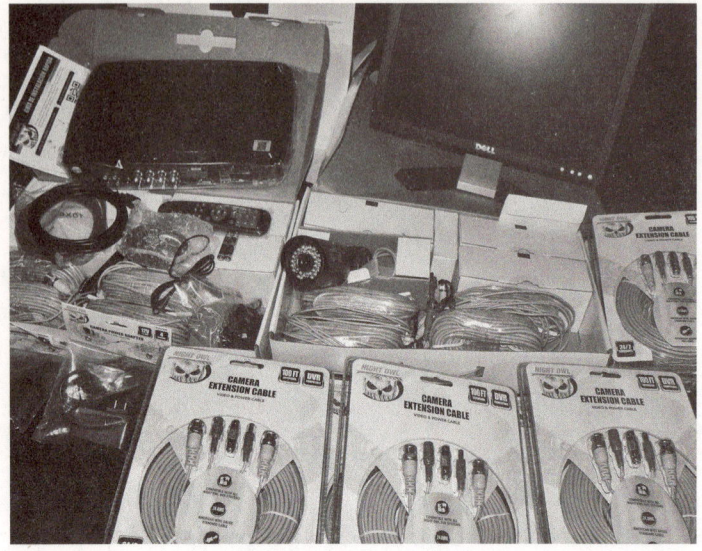

The new surveillance equipment.

If Norman was something spiritual, at least now we could monitor the activity properly.

Within a few days the surveillance system arrived, and we wasted no time setting it up.

A camera was placed on the front porch to document any unwanted visitors. The rest of the cameras were placed in the house. One in the kitchen, one in the living room, and one in the master bedroom where Norman resided.

Every few nights, we once again received an unwanted guest pounding on our front door—never to be there when we answered. Each and every time I would review the surveillance footage to find nothing out of the ordinary other than the dogs reacting.

Over the next few weeks, we noticed both our front door and bedroom door wide open upon returning home from a daily trip. Of course the first thing we did was review the surveillance.

To my surprise, the surveillance revealed the doors opening, but there was nobody there doing it. They were seemingly opening by themselves.

In the videos you can even see the dogs reacting to the doors opening and even, at times, walking backward as if they were afraid of something.

If you knew our dogs, when the front door opens, they fly out to play around in the yard. But not on these particular occasions.

They wanted nothing to do with those doorways. Norman and whatever came with him was beginning to get a lot more interesting.

More days came and went. Some without incident, some with more head scratching curiosity.

But I will never forget the day laughing became frightening instead of uplifting and positive.

That's a bold statement coming from a guy who spent the last twenty years in dark places interacting with ghosts.

Four

I never thought that I would be admitting that this was the most scared I had ever been in my life.

When you are alone and hear maniacal laughing with no logical source, it tends to get the butterflies flying in the stomach.

Christina was gone that morning, so it was just me and the four dogs. As predictable as I am, I was at my desk working on projects, going over case files, and documenting recent events.

It was somewhere around ten in the morning when my army of dogs started barking and growling at something outside in the front yard.

They were all standing at attention, looking out the living room windows.

I slowly walked out of the bedroom where my desk was located and crept up to the window just to see what they were so attentive to.

Considering recent events, I should have guessed nothing was going to be there.

Regardless, I immediately ran back into the bedroom where all of the gear was and grabbed a video camera.

I slowly, and very low to the ground, made my way to the kitchen where I could film out the window without being seen.

I began filming.

I could hear what sounded like a group of children laughing and carrying on, but I couldn't get a fix on them.

They sounded like they were right in the yard. But as you probably guessed, they weren't.

I ducked down and leaned against the cabinets, quietly calling my dogs into the kitchen with me. I ordered them to lie down and stay silent.

I stood up again to film more of the area the surveillance camera was blind to.

As I filmed out the window, I swear to you I heard from our bedroom a male laugh like he was amused.

Now it is very possible the laugh came from outside. But it is pretty easy to differentiate interior and exterior sounds.

Before I could think any more of it, the laughing continued. It was a very mischievous laugh.

I crept back to the bedroom as quietly as I possibly could.

Little did I know, at the same time all of this bizarre laughing was happening, a murder had taken place on our street.

I could now hear police sirens in the distance.

I took a quick look at Norman in the bedroom, then decided to walk outside to see what the commotion was about.

Meanwhile, while I was searching all around the exterior of my house for some clue that would solve the laughing, the murder on our street was becoming the talk of the town.

My girlfriend had heard the news and was unable to reach me. The news had traveled about someone being killed on our street, but the location was vague. She was concerned that someone could have been me.

She left work in a panic only to find the end of our road completely blocked off by the authorities.

After a few hours, they finally let her through, and when she saw me she was in tears.

I filled her in on everything I just told you. I was having a haunting experience at the house while somebody down the street was dying.

Was it all related? Will we ever know?

But I can't deny the knocks, and the laughter both inside and outside of our home.

And the truth cannot be denied that a man was just murdered and Norman found that quite funny.

My concern at that point was back to what was really going on inside our house.

Christina and I decided to sit down and discuss the recent events in relation to the paranormal field.

Invisible visitors, a mysterious woman, a death on our street, and the three-knock mystery.

My attention was focused more on the three knocks.

Every person knocks differently. Some knock soft, while others knock with confidence. Some tap out the rhythm to "Shave and a Haircut," while others do a constant knock.

I'm a constant knock kind of guy. I find it funny and annoying.

But all of these were in a series of three.

Every time: *knock knock knock.*

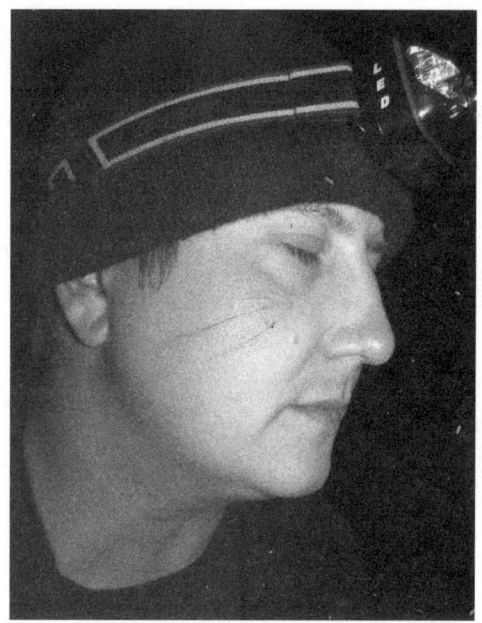
Three facial slashes following an attack.

The knocks always had the same timbre and the same amount of pauses in between the sequence.

In our line of work, anything in a series of three typically leans toward something demonic being the cause.

Whether it be the infamous Christianity-originated number of the beast, 666, or three scratches or bruises after a spiritual attack, to three knocks, it's commonly accepted to be demon related.

I prefer to call it heinous. What significance that has is beyond me, but in my experience that phenomena has always led to something harmful and evil.

During a previous case of ours involving an old plantation home, I was attacked and thrown down a flight of stairs. It was later revealed I had three slashes down the side of my face. Beyond a shadow of a doubt, whatever attacked me there was evil by any definition you wish to use.

I cover that case extensively in one of my previous books.

An evil entity doesn't always have to be labeled a demon. A murderer in real life is bound to be the same in the afterlife. Evil is evil any way you slice it. There doesn't necessarily need to be a religious connotation attached to it.

5

Take the Hint

It doesn't go without notice when you are alone in the house and something is thrown across a room, hitting you. Especially when that object is supposed to be a form of spiritual protection.

I was spending my day like I typically spend any other: at my desk in the bedroom.

It was fairly quiet with all of the dogs sleeping and only the sound of my keyboard clicking as I typed up a file.

The door to the bathroom was directly to the right of me as I sat and worked.

Suddenly my attention was piqued by what sounded like something falling in the bathroom. It sounded like an empty plastic cup hitting the linoleum.

I jumped up and opened the door thinking I was going to catch another rat or mouse. I was even thinking Little F was playing around in there.

I looked back over at my desk and saw Little F sleeping underneath it. So that definitely ruled her out.

There was nothing in the bathroom. The room was untouched.

I didn't give it a second thought, and I went back to work on the computer.

I left the bathroom door open so I could hear better just in case it happened again.

A few moments later the bathroom door slowly started to close. It shut so quietly I would not have even noticed if it wasn't for the dog on the floor beside me, growling.

I sat and watched the door come to a complete close while my dog growled faintly.

This door had never closed before on its own. The door was sturdy and heavy, didn't squeak, and was hard to close.

I opened the door back up and loaded up the surveillance footage from the bedroom to see if anything of interest popped out while the door was closing.

The only other observation was my dog lying down and then sitting up at attention when the door began to close.

So I once again went back to work at the desk thinking I was alone in the house.

As I was sitting there, I felt an object hit me in the back of the neck, and I instantly leapt up from my chair, looking all around the room for whoever threw it.

I was already on edge, considering how creepy the door closing and the dog growling was.

Object thrown as captured on surveillance.

Five

Discovering a statue.

When I looked down and discovered what had been thrown, I found myself standing there in shock and disbelief.

It was a one pound, hand-carved Korean protection statue.

Needless to say, it hurt when it hit me.

My heart was racing thinking somebody broke into the house and was attempting to attack me.

I picked up the statue and started walking around the bed to put it back on the shelf it came from.

There were two in the set, both identical in height at seven inches tall.

One was spiritually labeled to represent protection, and the other was to bring love.

Those seemed like such ironic things to be hit by, considering they are supposed to be protecting you.

With force, this statue had flown across the entire room with the purpose of hitting me.

I quickly checked the rest of the house, but there was nobody there.

Protection and love statues.

Now, with my head getting closer to accepting something paranormal was going on, I turned to the surveillance footage of the bedroom to see how exactly this happened.

It was amazing to watch a statue take flight from the bookshelf across the room and travel all the way to the back of my neck.

It was as if an invisible string had been pulled, drawing the statue to me. I must have watched it a dozen times. While I was reviewing the surveillance of the protection statue, I discovered an odd anomaly appear on the right-hand side of the screen.

Right at the moment the statue left the shelf, a very faint and transparent looking sphere about the size of a baseball appeared.

In sync, the sphere moved with the statue until disappearing right before the statue hit me. There was no explanation for what that was. That sphere appeared to have been what powered the throw. But how? Why?

Sphere appearing.

Nothing happened the rest of the day. It was just in and out, one time, like it was saying, "Hey, I'm here."

That evening Christina and I watched the surveillance footage over and over to figure it all out. But was that enough?

Knowing that the surveillance system was slowly becoming our best friend, I decided to name the cameras for easier referencing.

CH3, or Channel 3, became BED to signify the bedroom.

After labeling everything involved with the surveillance system, we went to bed.

I barely slept that evening. I just couldn't shake that feeling of the statue hitting me.

The following day was much like the day before it, with one dog on the bed and the others on the floor beside me. I went back to work early that morning.

A few more hours passed before a new picture was painted for me. I was typing away when I was interrupted by something falling behind me. I wasn't the only one disturbed.

Tank was on the bed sleeping. When I turned around in my chair to look for what fell, he was sitting up at attention, staring at the headboard.

We had been in the process of moving our room around, so the majority of haunted objects had been spread out throughout the room. At the moment, all that was on the headboard was a painting that Christina had made of a skull.

That painting was now lying on top of the pillows.

I stood up and placed the painting back in its respective spot on the headboard.

That painting had been sitting there for days without having been moved.

I squinted my eyes with an inquisitive look at Norman, who was sitting just beyond the painting.

I glanced at Tank and then glanced back at the surveillance system.

One more time I started reviewing the bedroom footage to see exactly what happened behind me when the painting fell.

My jaw dropped as I watched the painting sit itself upright from a leaned position.

A few seconds later it fell off of the headboard and down onto the pillows, causing Tank to jump up from his slumber.

That was the moment I turned around from my desk in the video.

As before, I watched the painting stand up then fall over and over.

How was this possible? I paced around and around the bedroom contemplating the events so far. I was feeling beyond uneasy at this point.

My attention was won.

I loaded the footage onto the computer and sent the file to Christina via the internet. She immediately opened the message and started watching the videos from her phone.

Take the Hint 67

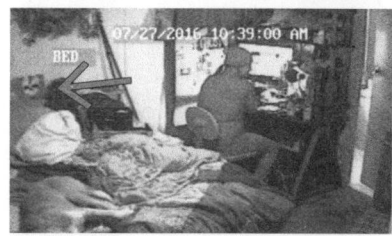

The painting moves on its own.

About ten minutes later she was calling me all excited and perplexed. The footage was hard to believe, but it was right there for us to see. As Christina went on and on about the unbelievable, I stared at Norman with his sly grin. Christina and I discussed all of the recent activity and what could possibly be causing it. At one point I said it was that damn doll. She agreed.

He had me in a trance during the entire phone call. It was unsettling that I couldn't stop staring at him, yet I was fully in control of myself. I was in mid-sentence to Christina when all of a sudden I'm knocked out of my trance and stunned by the sound of Christmas music playing.

My stomach sank.

You know that feeling when you are surprised and all of those tingles strike you inside? Without warning and without prompting, the speakers on my computer started playing a very somber version of "Deck the Halls."

There were no instruments in the song. It was simply a choir of children singing a more dismal and dissonant version. Without hesitation and almost laughing, Christina asked what I was listening to. I told her that "Deck the Halls" just started playing on the computer. Like me, she was in disbelief as she questioned me. She was convinced I was playing a joke.

But it was no joke.

I walked over to the computer in hopes of finding a plausible source of the music. I tried to search for any type of media player that could have been activated somehow. My computer was locked up and frozen. I wasn't able to do anything.

I couldn't type or click, open or close, search, or even shut it down. The entire operating system was inaccessible. I literally had to unplug the entire machine to power it down and stop the music. Christina was still on the other end of the phone, full of questions and, like me, curious as to how it happened. I plugged the computer back in and rebooted it.

Once it returned to normal operations, there was nothing to be found. No computer virus or anything to explain the phantom music.

I had never heard that version of the song in my life, nor would there have been any reason for me to even have it on the computer. The music never played again.

A Christmas song of all things. As if any song playing with wasn't enough.

To me that was all I needed to finally come to the realization our house was haunted and had been ever since bringing Norman there. I shared those thoughts with Christina as I recounted the story of the Christmas Eve fire and the unborn twin. All clues were leading to Norman.

Before the phone call ended, I told Christina I was going to run some tests on our new friend to see if there was any reason for spiritual concern. I guess a hit in the head was exactly what I needed to take the hint. The Korean statue and the skull painting.

Interestingly enough, both occurrences happened at nearly the same time, between ten and eleven in the morning. I couldn't come to any conclusions as to why, but the similarities between days were worth noting.

I hung up the phone and placed Norman on the center of the bed. I placed him with his back against the pillow to keep him from falling forward or backward.

He was very top heavy due to his thick, plastic head and completely soft body. He had no endoskeleton, and the only thing actually inside him was the mechanism that plays his voice when the string is pulled.

I set up a video camera on a tripod to document all of the tests, with the focal point directly on the doll. My plan was to conduct three simple tests to determine anything paranormal. The first test consisted of measuring ionic energy around him. This was accomplished by placing three devices designed to detect ionic energy on and around Norman's body. I placed one directly on top of his head and the other two at his feet.

These devices were equipped with a small antenna and a blue light at the top. If any ionic energy was present around him, the blue light would power on, notifying me of the environment change.

Sure enough, the devices lit up like a Christmas tree. All three would flicker their blue lights off and on every few seconds randomly all around Norman.

There were no electrical components inside of Norman. That fact instantly ruled out any logical causes of the energy bursts.

The detection of ionic energy went on and on with no signs of ever stopping. Every living thing has ionic energy. I could wave my hand over one of those devices and it would light up.

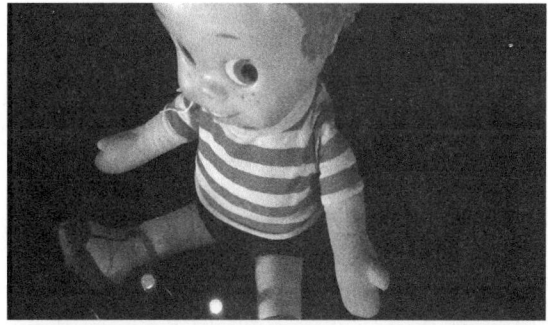

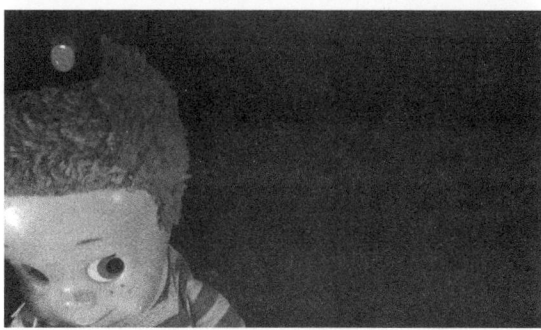

Ionic testers on Norman.

So was I staring at something that was actually living in some form or way?

After documenting twenty minutes of this, I removed the devices to begin another test.

Next I ran simple electromagnetic field tests to see if he omitted another form of energy.

Every electrical device gives off an electromagnetic field (EMF). A refrigerator, a microwave, and even something as small as an digital watch will give off detectable fields.

All that ever really differs is how high or low the EMF read actually is. The higher the read, the stronger the field.

It is believed in the science of paranormal research that electromagnetic fields are used as an energy source for a spirit. This gives them the ability to speak, move objects, or even manifest.

With that under consideration, the higher the field, the stronger the spirit will become.

The readings discovered on Norman were much higher than that of an average refrigerator. He was sitting in the middle of the bed with nothing electrical in him or within six feet of him.

When something can't be explained, we call that paranormal. Like the ionic energy test, I logged the information in disbelief.

I was two for three so far with my testing, and now it was time to start monitoring his temperature. To do this I used a standard temperature gun that omits a laser. It will give you an accurate temperature read wherever the laser is hitting.

I shot it directly onto Norman. At first, he registered at seventy-four degrees Fahrenheit.

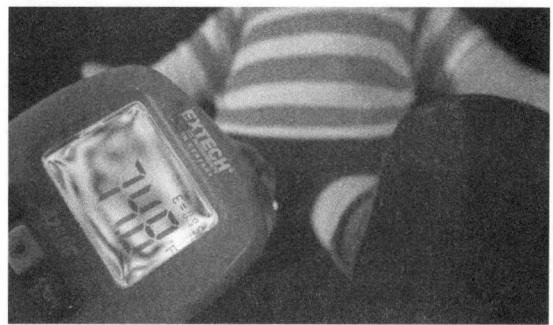

Initial temperature.

Then his temperature started to drop drastically.

Within sixty seconds, Norman's body temperature went from seventy-four degrees to fifty-four degrees. I just witnessed and documented a temperature degree drop on an inanimate object. There was without a doubt something spiritual residing in Norman.

All it took was three simple tests with three simple conclusions to defy everyday, modern science and prove to me something abnormal was happening with the doll.

Five

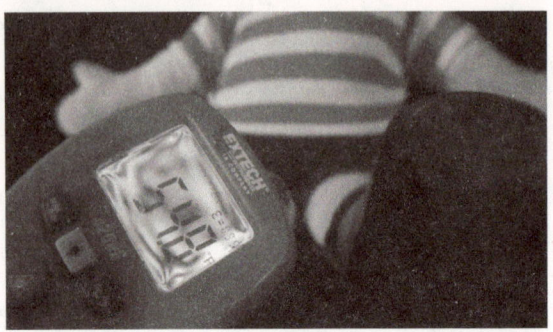

Drastic drop in temperature.

The activity from Norman had been escalating since the day we brought him into the house. For some strange reason, I had this feeling that Norman was self-aware, that he knew what I knew. If there was a consciousness in the body of that doll, he would have been watching my every move. With that being said, it is very hard to be one step ahead when all plastic eyes are constantly on you.

Christina arrived home that evening and I shared with her all of the test results as she watched the video of the trials.

We both agreed that Norman was possessed with something, and from that point we both agreed to find out what exactly that was. This opened Christina up a little bit. She decided to confide to me something she had never told me the next morning.

The narrative of this story was about to change drastically upon learning of yet another disturbing coincidence involving the spirit inside Norman.

And maybe, at this juncture, using the word *coincidence* is the wrong choice.

6

Duality

Christina has five children. The four boys—Blake, Cody, Matthew, and Asheston—are all grown up and out on their own, leaving Hannah, the one and only girl, at age fifteen, still living with us.

However, I would come to find out that Hannah was supposed to have a twin brother. Trust me, I didn't want to believe it either. But it's all true—hospital records prove it.

We were lying awake in bed one morning when I noticed Christina was not acting like herself. I can always tell when something is wrong with her: she just shuts down.

You know? You get the "I'm fine," and as we all know, that means "You better keep asking."

I kept at her and eventually she shared a story I had yet to hear, a story that opened my eyes to the haunting we were experiencing.

Six

Christina became pregnant again in October 2000. In January 2001, Christina's life was turned upside down after getting in a terrible car accident. But frankly, you can't call it an accident because that word implies nobody was at fault. Somebody literally ran her off the road and headfirst into a tree.

Still to this day, the oncoming vehicle that crossed into her lane at high speed has not been identified.

I can only assume a drunk driver carelessly veered into her lane, forcing her to make a quick decision. This ultimately placed her off the road, into the woods, and wrapped around a tree.

The guy saw the accident but chose to keep on going. Sometimes the most frightening things in the world are selfish, uncompassionate cowards you can barely call human beings. The guy is a murderer as far as I am concerned.

It wasn't until the next morning that she was discovered by a passing vehicle.

She had been unconscious all night and trapped inside the crushed remains of the car. Emergency responders used the Jaws of Life to cut her out of the vehicle. Christina was immediately rushed to the hospital.

Doctors feared the worst, considering she was pregnant. A crash that extreme rarely ends well for the victims. However, other than minor cuts and bruises, she was fine. But there was some bad news to deliver. The doctor informed her that she had lost one of her babies in the crash.

Christina questioned the doctor's news because of the way he worded the terrible news—"one of your babies." Christina thought she was only carrying one baby. But the doctor revealed to her that she was in fact pregnant with twins.

One was a girl, and the other was a boy. The girl survived, and the boy tragically did not.

I'm not medically educated by any definition, though I do hold a degree in psychology.

My expertise is evaluating behavior and mental processes. Which, believe me, drives my friends and family crazy.

Good choice of word there, huh? Crazy.

So I often turn to Christina when it comes to wanting to absorb some medical knowledge. Occasionally I pick my mother's brain as well, who has retired from the medical field.

What happened to Christina after the accident is called vanishing twin syndrome (VTS). First recognized in 1945, VTS occurs when a twin disappears from the uterus during pregnancy. This is typically a result of a miscarriage.

Occasionally, a twin can vanish in which no medical reason for the disappearance can be determined.

The dead fetal tissue is absorbed by the other twin, the placenta, or even the mother. It's like a magic trick. Which is why the syndrome is often referred to "vanishing twin."

Six

Vanishing twin syndrome sounds ghostly enough as it is, let alone relating this story to the history of Norman and our current situation.

My girlfriend lost a son that she never knew she was even going to have in the first place. I can only imagine the emotional overload that was at that time.

It was good news, however, to learn that the surviving daughter was healthy as can be and suffered from no health issues deriving from the car wreck.

On July 5, 2001, Christina went into labor. Hannah was born without issue. And she was born without the brother nobody knew she was even going to have.

And fifteen years later, Hannah finally learned the truth of her own birth and her brother's death. Fifteen years later, that brother arrived.

Learning that my girlfriend shared the same story as the spirit that resided in Norman and the surviving sister was a little more than disturbing. This newfound knowledge lent more credence to our theories on the haunted doll and his motives.

We now had two mothers who were pregnant with twins, lost their boys, and gave birth to girls. We now had two mothers with a daughter who ended up with Matty, or as we now know him, Norman.

I just couldn't help but keep putting all of the little pieces of the puzzle together.

It was amazing. It was perfect. It was like a screenplay full of twists and turns.

There was a thirty-nine-year difference between the original twin tragedy and this one. The original birth took place in July 1962. Hannah's birth took place in July 2001. We discovered the doll at the antique shop in July.

This was uncanny.

At the time of writing this, I turned thirty-nine years old, and Norman was attempting to erase me.

This was like a bad case of the best synchronicity one could ask for.

Where was Carl Jung when you needed him? Carl Jung was a psychoanalyst that first introduced the concept of synchronicity in the early 1920s. He explained synchronicity as events that were "meaningful coincidences" if they happened with no causal relationship. He further added that these occurrences with no causal relationship held more validity by definition if they appeared to be meaningfully related.

That could not explain our current situation any better.

Nor Christina or myself had any causal relationship with the original tragedy in 1962, the girl, or the doll, yet what was happening to us fell firmly within the realm of being meaningfully related.

Our lives were haunted by the spirit trapped inside a doll. Not only were we reliving his story, but he was attempting to rewrite it.

So the mystery kept unfolding. Only it wasn't a mystery at this point; this was life, in whatever form it was choosing to take.

With everything going on inside our home, there needed to be no secrets. The haunting, the fear, Norman, and history rewriting itself left no room for any of us to hide anything.

You always hear people say they are haunted by the past.

With us, we were haunted by the past and the present and whatever the future was going to bring with our sinister, smiling little pal.

The holy grail of evidence was coming, and it was going to be handed to me by a couple of kids.

7

The Children Speak

The boy worried me. He had a special, uncontrollable curiosity about that doll. He had an attachment that seemed inseparable, like a boy expressing love for his favorite dog. I often observed him sitting and staring at the doll for moments on end like he was in a trance or even possessed himself. This was the same thing I had experienced before.

If it was not for my girlfriend's grandchildren I would have never discovered the most captivating piece of evidence in favor of proving Norman was alive.

In fact, in my twenty years of paranormal research, it remains one of the most remarkable things I have ever seen captured on film.

I babysat the grandchildren often so it was nothing for me to have a handful of what I call the gremlins at the house.

They all call me Grandpa even though Christina and I aren't married yet. But I don't mind it. I was Grandpa Stephen, and even better yet, I was the coolest grandpa. Those are their words, not mine. I won't argue with that.

Their grandmother and their soon-to-be grandfather chase ghosts, and they thought that was just the coolest thing in the world. I can't wait for career day when I am asked to go to their school and speak. I'm sure I will receive some phone calls that night!

Back to the point at hand.

This particular day I was watching Liam and Lyndsay, the children of Christina's son Matthew. They are two characters all their own, but they have to be the easiest children in the world to babysit. At ages eight and ten, they were both fairly self-sufficient and glued to their handheld gaming systems and tablets.

They occasionally glance up at the television to the cartoons I have going, though I probably watch more of the cartoons than they do.

Lyndsay is an extreme storyteller, and you can't help but laugh at the lengths she will go to avoid trouble. I could write an entire book on just that.

So when she tells me she saw Norman walk across the bedroom floor, I had to just nod and say, "Oh wow, that's cool." Which really translates into, "Yeah right, Lyndsay, I believe that."

That particular day, Matt dropped the two kids off at the house around eight thirty in the morning and he was expected to pick them up around two thirty that afternoon.

They play their games while I work on my projects, and we all pretty much just stay in the bedroom because that's where my office is.

Once in a while they break away from their games with curiosity as to what I am doing on the computer. I show them various pieces of footage from my investigations, which they think is really cool.

But because of that, it's hard to believe their ghost stories. You know, you have to consider that matter of influence.

That morning was the first time Liam and Lyndsay noticed Norman. He was sitting on the headboard at the time.

Liam worried me because he instantly gravitated toward the doll and pulled it from the headboard. Of all the things he could have grabbed. A mechanical cat, a Raggedy Ann, a Mogwai, a black cat, a crying porcelain doll, etcetera.

All of those things he was used to. He had asked about them before.

It had to be Norman though.

There beckoned more curiosity in me. A real-life child choosing Norman, who has the spirit of a boy and a mentality of a wise old man inside of him.

He immediately started asking questions about him, like what his name was and where did he come from. I kept my answers brief. "His name is Norman and we found him at a store."

It took no time for Liam to notice the cord on Norman's back and of course, give it a tug. Nothing but more creepy and garbled phrases came out, like a demon trying to mumble Latin.

Liam even said that it was creepy and he didn't want it anymore. So I took the doll and placed him up on the dresser and went back to work on the computer.

Lyndsay was sitting in the chair directly in front of our surveillance monitor and Liam was lying on the bed.

Liam was playing with his handheld gaming system and Lyndsay sat with her tablet.

Like I said, the television was airing cartoons, the kids were preoccupied, and it appeared our day was going to consist of just that.

I would say maybe an hour had passed when Lyndsay pointed out something rather shocking. She turned around in her chair, now sitting on her knees and facing Liam on the bed.

"Grandpa Stephen, the doll moved!"

"What are you talking about?" I asked, looking at her.

She immediately pointed to the bed, and, sure enough, there sat Norman in the center of the pillows at the top of the bed.

Liam was lying on his stomach facing the television, so he had no idea what had happened.

The problem I had was that my back was turned to all of them. I was facing my computer, so it wasn't that hard to fathom Liam pulling a little trickery.

Maybe he jumped off of the bed, grabbed Norman, and placed him on the pillows.

So I decided to play their little game.

At this point Liam had turned around and saw Norman, and I asked him if he had placed him on the bed. He said no.

I immediately went to the surveillance.

Now this is the part that really, really upset me.

As I reviewed the time between Norman being placed on the dresser to the point he appeared on the bed, there was a piece missing. The footage jumped in time. The surveillance footage played fine up until he showed up on the bed. It was quick, but the footage immediately went from Norman being on the dresser to appearing on the pillows in the middle of the bed.

All that was in between was a quick black screen. Did Norman do something to prevent me from actually having hard-copy footage of him physically moving? Was it just bad timing and a random glitch?

Considering everything that has happened in the house since he came through that front door, I wasn't buying the glitch theory.

One second he was on the dresser and the next second he was on the bed.

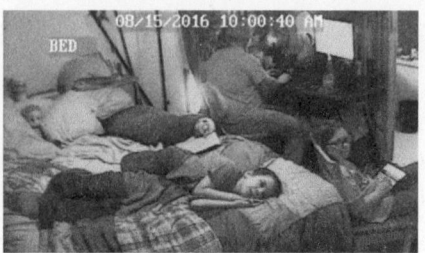

Norman staring at Liam.

There was no proof as to whether or not Liam moved Norman or whether he moved himself.

I was a little more than frustrated, but I just sat back down at the computer to continue working on my project.

Another hour passed and I needed a break from the computer. I told the kids to stay right where they were as I left the room. I could still hear them, but hey, you know kids?

I expected to come out of the bathroom to find random status updates on one of my social networks. You can't trust the hands of your grandkids.

Instead, the children remained in their respective locations, until Lyndsay started screaming and pounding on the bathroom door. Needless to say I was caught with my pants down. I started yelling through the door at Lyndsay and asking what was wrong.

She was so believable in her delivery. She sounded freaked out. Lyndsay said that Norman was on my desk.

With that being said, I shot out the bathroom door as quick as I could. Sure enough, there sat Norman, sitting to the left of my computer screen.

I asked both of them if they had seen him move from the bed. They had not.

She said she just turned around and saw him on my desk. She said she did not like that thing at all.

Once again, I sat down at the surveillance system to see what would hopefully confirm what the kids had been saying.

I started reviewing the footage, starting back where Norman magically appeared on the bed.

There I was sitting at the computer, Lyndsay in her chair, and Liam still lying on his belly facing the television.

After about fifteen minutes of watching the footage, just about every profane word you can imagine came spewing out of my mouth.

That was followed by Lyndsay yelling at her grandpa for saying such things, but I could not believe what I was seeing.

I stopped the footage and walked out into the living room for a minute, thinking I was losing my mind, or maybe I was becoming a victim of influence myself.

Maybe I was just hallucinating or seeing what I wanted to see.

After collecting myself, I walked back into the bedroom and was instantly greeted with overexcited children wanting to know what I had seen.

This time there was no glitch. This time Norman wanted me to see what he could do, and I think he did just to seal the deal as to who exactly was in control.

In the footage you see me at the desk with my back turned to the children who remained in their respective locations.

Norman was sitting in the center of the pillows on the bed, just like before.

The footage showed Norman physically moving. His head turned to the left, which was in my direction. It was like he wanted to see what I was doing or wanted to make sure I couldn't see what he was doing.

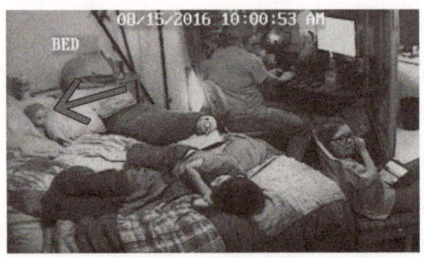

Norman turns his head.

Norman saw me as the threat, I guess. He was focusing on Liam. I just wish I knew why.

While I was sitting oblivious to what was going on behind me, Liam turned around and looked at Norman. He saw Norman moving his head and looking around.

Norman's head continues to move.

Liam started smiling.

His reaction was very off-putting.

What eight-year-old kid doesn't jump up screaming at the sight of a doll he previously called creepy when witnessing it actually moving.

Instead, still smiling, Liam turned back around and continued to watch his show.

As if that wasn't unsettling enough, Norman turned his head back toward Liam who was still lying flat on the bed facing the television.

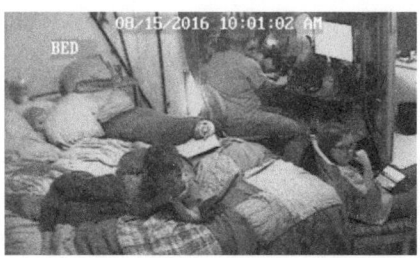

Liam notices Norman moving.

This is where the footage defied all rationality.

Norman looked down.

Why is that so important?

His design does not allow for the head to move up or down. His head can only move left and right.

But the footage did not stop there.

A few moments later, Liam sat up, turned around, and moved closer to Norman.

Sitting in an Indian style fashion, all he did was stare at Norman.

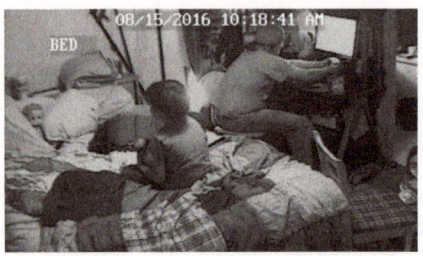

Liam in Norman's trance.

I knew that feeling all too well.

Liam was experiencing the same trance-like state that I experienced when Norman took control.

But after about ten minutes, something changed in Liam. He became angry.

He removed himself from the bed and went over to be closer to his sister. From there he continued to stare at Norman.

Eventually Liam started grabbing random toys in the room and throwing them at the doll. He was a pretty good aim, too, considering just about every throw hit Norman directly.

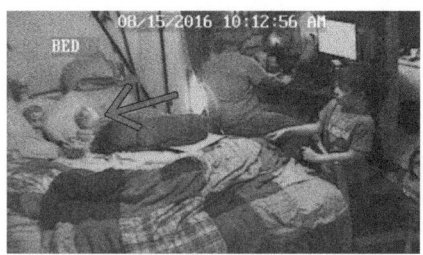

Liam throwing toys.

Shortly after what I can only guess was Liam's way of coping with a possible fear by throwing stuff at Norman, he proceeded to get back on the bed.

He did the same thing as before and sat directly in front of Norman before smacking him across the face and knocking him over on his side.

Then Liam returned to lying flat on his stomach facing the television.

Lyndsay had been so preoccupied with her gaming device that she was unaware that Norman had become animated just a few feet from the both of us. The two were now watching the surveillance footage with me. Liam was doing his best to recap his actions.

He claimed he could hear Norman talking and that Norman was saying very bad things. Although I could never get out of Liam what exactly that was, other than the doll wanted to hurt somebody.

With all of the excitement of having real footage of Norman's activity, I had nearly forgotten about my disappearance into the bathroom and Norman's alleged jump to my desk.

I sped to that section of the footage, but this time there was another glitch.

Just like when he moved from the dresser to the bed, the screen went blank for a moment as he reappeared on my desk.

I wasn't taking any chances with that footage. I immediately hooked up a flash drive and loaded the video onto the portable storage device. From the flash drive, I then loaded the captures onto my computer for further analysis.

I watched it over and over and over on my computer.

I opened it up in some top-notch video editing software, where I was able to clean up the video a bit and zoom in on the actual movement of the doll. The video footage was already high definition, so zooming in did not degrade the quality much at all.

I immediately started emailing the footage to colleagues of mine who specialize in demonology, possession, and haunted objects.

It took a few days, but their responses were just as overwhelming as mine. In fact, they wrote the foreword and epilogue to this book. They were just as intrigued and just as wary as I was when it came to the intentions of Norman. Of course, I also sent the footage to Christina via email, and like before, she was calling me overly excited. She honestly thought it was a prank. She thought it was staged.

The surveillance footage was so good that it really was difficult to believe it was authentic.

I didn't blame Christina for questioning it one bit. I would have done the same thing.

Her first assumption was that me and Matt had somehow staged it. However, I assured her that Matt was not there at the time. It was just me, the children, and the dogs.

She expressed her impatience and excitement. Christina could not wait to get home to see these videos on a screen much bigger than a cell phone.

Footage like this is something you see in the movies. Actually having a hard copy on video of a haunted doll coming to life is a remarkable privilege.

Some investigators and researchers work their entire lives for proof like this, and we obtained it because two children brought it to my attention. I would have never believed the kids' story if it weren't for the surveillance, which was running seven days a week.

But now there is nothing to question. There is nothing to believe. When you believe something you accept it as being true. That doesn't necessarily mean it is. Belief and fact are two different things; what we had here was pure fact.

Hours later Matt returned to the house to pick up Lyndsay and Liam, and of course they beat me to the punch in telling him what happened with Norman. He was in total disbelief as expected, but I spoke up and told him it was all true. He immediately demanded to see the videos.

I showed Matt the footage, and I swear if his mouth stayed gaping open for too much longer he would have started drooling.

He couldn't grasp it either. It also bothered him how his son Liam seemed to be afraid yet attached to the doll. Liam even asked if he could take it home. Both Matt and I responded simultaneously with a resounding "no!" Matt asked if his mom had seen it yet, and I told him I sent it to her and she thought we staged it.

But proving Matt and I didn't stage it was easy. With all of the time-stamped surveillance throughout the house, it would be easy to show Christina footage from the time Matt went out the door to the time he came back through it hours later.

Once Christina arrived home, I showed her everything. The beauty of the surveillance system is you can watch all cameras at once. It was easy to see there was no manipulation. It was all right there for all of us to see.

This was the perfect setup. This was the perfect piece of evidence that could not be denied. This was all that needed to be seen. No more questions. No more guessing. Without a doubt we had something very powerful in our home. There was no more trying to explain things away. Norman was alive. Norman was physically able to move.

As exciting as that was, it made me sick to my stomach.

If Norman could throw objects, physically move, affect electrical devices, and speak, what else was he capable of doing?

Knowing at that moment all of this had been real and that all of this had sinister intent behind it left no question that our house was no longer safe. It was indeed haunted with a malevolent entity.

I could feel it in my heart that matters were about to become a whole lot worse. And I could feel it in my heart that this wouldn't have a happy ending.

There was no more need for the brain, or my experience, or Christina's experience in the field of the paranormal. Sure my colleagues shared some appreciated insight, but they weren't the ones living this nightmare.

I was torn. I lived my life for this. But in the past, I was able to leave it somewhere else in most cases. Sometimes it would come home with me and I dealt with that. I've had my share of some horrible spiritual attachments, but nothing like this.

Every time the grandchildren would come over, they went right to Norman to start their questions to me. They would want to know what else he had done. They would grab my attention and tell me he moved again.

Sometimes it was on surveillance, sometimes it wasn't.

Our home instantly went from a happy house to a full state of emergency.

This mess was now affecting our grandchildren. Hell, it was affecting our lifestyle.

That footage became the talk of the family for days and days. Our phone wouldn't stop ringing with questions that we had very few answers to.

But who do you call upon when you're supposed to be the experts on such matters?

911

How do you, with a straight face, tell a sheriff that your house is haunted by a spirit that's trapped inside a fifty-year-old doll?

How can you honestly look him in the eye when he is standing on your porch at three in the morning and say, "Sorry, it was that damn ghost again!" The answer is you don't. At least not at that moment.

Unless I wanted law enforcement thinking I was crazy or pulling a prank, I was keeping my mouth shut concerning the supernatural.

But I had to tell them something and I had to tell them something that showed an effort was being made to rationalize what can be considered illegal.

Depending on what state you live in, 911 emergency calls that are phony, staged, misrepresented, a product of a prank, or unrelated to an actual emergency can result in hefty fines.

So why am I telling you this? Have you ever heard of phantom calls?

Until we had our unwanted experiences with the telephone, I had never heard of such a thing. I did some research and discovered that the National Emergency Number Association reports that phantom wireless calls account for up to 70 percent of all 911 calls in some areas in the United States.

Now to clarify, "phantom calls" are simply calls that were either dialed by mistake or the result of some sort of glitch.

For us, phantom calls meant something entirely different.

Our phone, which was a landline, called 911 in the middle of the night not once but six times on six different occasions.

It was easy to speculate, especially when attempting to put all of the puzzle pieces together concerning Norman, that his original owner was six years old at the time of the fire in 1968.

It was a stretch, but with all of my experience in the field of paranormal research, taking everything into consideration was a must.

What one person might feel is irrelevant could actually be the key factor in solving a paranormal investigation.

After further research into the National Emergency Number Association, I learned that the majority of phantom calls come from cell phones. They explain away these mistakes as speed-dial errors—the infamous butt dial.

However, that was not the case with us.

Although we both had cell phones, our mystery calls were being made directly from the cordless phone in our bedroom. This phone, as I said earlier, was the one and only landline in our house.

The unsettling part about all of this was the fact it was happening right underneath our noses, and in plain view. The house phone was in our bedroom.

There were no speed-dial keys on that phone, nor was there ever an opportunity in the middle of the night for the phone to be in a position to butt dial.

This phone had to be picked up off of its charging base, the "talk" button pressed, and 9-1-1 physically dialed to make these calls possible.

In addition to that, the phone was five feet from the floor on our television.

It definitely wasn't something a sixteen-inch doll could reach. Yet, somehow emergency calls were being placed, and we had no explanation for it.

The first night it happened just about gave me a heart attack.

It was around three fifteen in the morning when an intimidating pounding literally made me fall out of bed in a panic.

Along with the knocking came our army of dogs sounding off in unison.

I immediately knew it was somebody at the door. My only concern was that another addict was mistaking the house for our now-behind-bars drug dealer from next door. The demanding-sounding knocking wasn't too comforting either. I then glanced over at the monitor for the surveillance, and to my surprise, I saw flashing lights from a patrol car, an ambulance, and an officer standing at our front door.

I couldn't ignore it, and at this point Christina was wide awake too.

So at that moment me and my groggy bed-head self had to answer the door. I calmed the dogs down and opened the door to greet the officer. We both had confused looks on our faces as he asked me if everything was alright. I assured him there wasn't any problem and we were all sleeping soundly until his arrival. He told me a 911 call came from our house around three and they were dispatched to investigate.

He said whoever called said nothing, not a word, and didn't even make a sound. All the dispatcher could hear was static fading in and out.

The sheriff said it sounded like a radio when you are not quite locked in on a clear station. He added that when the dispatcher attempted to call our number back, she was met with a rapid busy signal.

I immediately apologized for the inconvenience and waste of tax dollars, considering we did not really have an emergency. But the officer still insisted he do a walk-through of the house just to be sure. He said it was standard procedure.

He explained to me that sometimes there are hostage situations and people are instructed not to tell the police it's unsafe in the house, just like you see in the movies.

I let him in and he did a full sweep of our home and left shortly after. Christina and I didn't think much of it that first time and went immediately back to bed.

A few days later, the same thing happened again. Yet another mysterious, unmanned phone call to emergency services was made. This time it was about two thirty in the morning.

Like the time before, the same chain of events occurred.

I jumped out of bed with my heart racing. Christina leaped up to a sitting position, and we both immediately looked at the surveillance monitor.

The scene was almost identical to the previous mishap.

Once again, the officer reported no caller on the other line. The 911 dispatcher was left to send out help without knowing if there was an emergency or not.

After undergoing the same routine with law enforcement, we decided to sit down behind the surveillance system to review the footage at the time the call was made. Our phone was clearly visible on the camera monitoring the bedroom. We reviewed the surveillance from approximately two in the morning until we saw the police arrive.

The phone did not move once. It was never picked up and it certainly wasn't used to make a call.

This was really bizarre.

It was hard to say what the real cause of this phenomena was. Nothing like this had ever happened in the past, so this incident was isolated and once again the fingers were pointed at Norman.

But something had to explain it. Why 911? Why call the police? If there was sinister intent behind this, what was the point?

As in the past, concluding that Norman was involved in some way wasn't going to satisfy me just yet.

This entire time, Norman had been sitting on my desk completely on the other side of the bedroom from where the phone sat. The last good piece of evidence we had of activity concerning Norman was with the grandchildren and those surveillance captures. But that was weeks ago.

I decided to move our peculiar doll closer to the phone just to see if maybe something different would happen.

At this point, what did we have to lose other than another night of disturbed sleep?

Two days later brought us a third phantom call to 911 and a third visit from our old pal the sheriff.

I was up and to the door so fast I never even noticed Norman lying on the bedroom floor because I was so preoccupied with the light show outside. This time the sheriff stayed for a while.

I think he thought at this point that we were either making the calls as a prank or there was something else at play, such as a glitch.

He left us his card this time with instructions to call him if we could think of any reason as to why our house had called 911 three times.

I got the feeling from him he was expecting us to come clean.

After he left, Christina pointed out that Norman was on the bedroom floor. We instantly went to reviewing the surveillance.

At the exact time the sheriff claimed the call came from our home, Norman fell off of the television and hit the floor.

Was that just a coincidence?

I thought at first that me jumping up to answer the door caused enough shaking in the room to make him fall, but the surveillance showed otherwise. Surveillance does not lie.

At least we didn't see Norman pick up the phone and make a call. That would have been the money shot.

The next day, and this time it was actually during the day, the officer returned to talk with us a bit more.

Unfortunately, Christina was off running errands so it was just me and the sheriff sitting at the kitchen table, admittedly awkwardly at first.

I mean, what do you say to a cop that has been to your house now four times in less than a week for unknown reasons?

Eight

But discussion ensued regardless.

He asked me about the murder that took place on our street and I showed him the video of all the laughing from that day.

After breaking the ice, he asked me about paranormal investigating. I was bewildered at first that he even knew what I did for a living. He wanted to pick my brain. After the second call to 911, he ran a background check on both Christina and me.

By whatever means he went about that, he discovered that I was an author who chronicled my paranormal investigations, that my work was cataloged in the Library of Congress.

He was quite curious about that.

So we shared some stories back and forth, which was not something I had seen coming.

He told me a few stories of his own involving his grandfather and calls he answered in the past involving home invasions in which no one was there.

The guy seemed to be a believer. I told him that I had experience with the same thing concerning a restaurant named Poogan's Porch Restaurant in Charleston, South Carolina, which I had investigated.

There are actual police reports of officers responding to intruders of the restaurant, yet nobody is ever there upon arrival. After the small talk, I started to wonder what his real motive was.

I don't know if he was waiting for me to say that I felt something supernatural was calling the police or not, but I did decide to show him some things I felt he would find interesting.

I showed him the surveillance footage with the grandchildren and he kept asking me if that was actually real or not. The look on his face was a curious one indeed.

I of course showed him the doll and how it was placed by the phone now as an experiment.

This prompted me to bring up how the doll was later found on the floor following the call.

After filling him in on the beginning of our experiences with Norman to the present, he advised I call the phone company to have them look into the constant, unwarranted, and mysterious calls.

He even added that I should write a book about the doll. All I could do was laugh, considering I was already in the middle of it.

He told me if he was ever called in on something that bordered the strange, he would let me know. I thought that was pretty cool.

He said he liked my style and attention to detail. I told him assisting the police would be an honor and an awesome experience if that day would ever come.

Shortly after the sheriff left, I called our phone provider and filled them in on the strange happenings and requested a technician for an inspection.

They told me over the phone that nothing out of the ordinary was standing out, but they did verify the three calls to 911 and the exact times they took place.

You guessed it: the technician arrived and found absolutely nothing wrong with our setup, wiring, or service.

I swear he must have been brothers with the exterminator, because he found nothing either. Yet there was definitely something.

Every action has a reaction, which means there had to be an action to begin with.

But nobody could figure it out. Over the next week, three more calls in the middle of the night went out to emergency services. Round and round we went with their arrival, and no explanation from either party. The phantom calls stopped with six, however, and it never happened again.

Six calls, on six different occasions with no caller, no return calls possible, and only static on the other end. Strange indeed.

Sometimes answers are right in front of your face and sometimes they are not. But I think the phantom calls were meant to act as a prelude to upcoming events, ones that would actually require a 911 call.

9

He Killed

I will never forget that morning. It was a Thursday and I was the first one out of bed. Christina was still fast asleep and so was Hannah.

Just like every morning, I made my way to the front door to let the dogs out.

Instead of opening the door to North Carolina sunshine and humidity, I was opening the door to a funeral procession.

Typically the dogs all bolt out the door in a herd so they can run and play like little maniacs in the yard. However, this morning changed my perspective on everything.

I opened the door and they started to run, but then stopped dead in their tracks, looking down at something lying on the porch. All four dogs were surrounding whatever it was, blocking my view.

I finally gave the command to go take care of their business and when they moved that's when I saw it.

There was Little F...or at least what was left of him. There were parts of him everywhere.

My little inseparable buddy had become every definition of separable. My poor little cat had been torn to shreds. I wish I could sugarcoat this part of the story, but it was a gory mess. In fact I had never seen anything like it, outside a horror film. I have seen animal attacks many times before, but they were nothing like this. Blood drenched the entire area.

It was as if something grabbed all four of his limbs and pulled with a great force in opposite directions in one solid motion.

There was anger and motive and something personal behind this attack.

I slowly turned around and walked back into the house to wake Christina. I woke her up and told her to follow me. There was something she had to see.

We walked out to the porch and once her eye made contact, her jaw dropped. She was speechless.

I broke the silence by questioning how this was even possible. Little F was an indoor cat and never once was allowed outside. The only way he could have found himself outside would be with door left open. And nobody did that.

Well, at least not one of us.

Christina examined his remains. There were no bite or claw marks on the body and she learned his rib cage had been completely crushed.

What a way to start the day.

I cleaned up Little F and Christina and I spent the morning digging a grave and putting him to rest. We wanted him off of the porch before her daughter could see what had happened.

While I was removing his parts from the porch I noticed extreme claw marks in the wood. This only made the situation more disturbing. Little F went down with a fight.

I took a picture of the claw marks after I removed most of the mess. I did not want a photograph of Little F like that because it was an image I never wanted to see again.

There was much hate and disdain behind the attack on Little F. A normal animal attack rarely displays a purpose beyond defense or the circle of life. He was not killed for food nor was he murdered for survival. He was simply destroyed for the sole purpose of being obliterated. Little F was the messenger literally killed. Even considering paranormal animal attacks; a carnal creature used as a vessel and puppeteered by a malevolent force still is at the will of the limitations of flesh and blood. Supernatural or not, there was a motive behind this event that no living animal has the capability of understanding or deliberating. It was a sad moment to say the least. He was my little buddy.

Large claw marks in the wood.

The last we had seen of him was prior to midnight when I got up to use the restroom. This would mean that at some point between midnight and seven in the morning, Little F left us.

Following his burial, Christina and I decided to review the surveillance from the night to see if we could pinpoint how Little F escaped, or was purposely let out.

We learned that at around three thirty in the morning the front door opened, seemingly by itself. This would have meant the door was unlocked, then opened, and then finally shut after Little F exited.

More claw marks.

We can only assume he was murdered shortly after that. But we couldn't say for sure what did it. Maybe it was another animal from outside. However, we can say that no animal opened that door.

Tension was starting to boil in our home.

When you know you can't sleep peacefully at night because your front door keeps opening and you know that something is willing to kill what you care about—well, it is easy and frankly appropriate to become unhinged. At this point, the activity had peaked once again. My beloved cat was dead. To add insult to injury, it was my birthday. My thirty-ninth birthday to be exact. This wasn't precisely the gift I wanted.

This made me start to think about what else could happen. How far would Norman go to make his point? The evening was closing in and nobody said much of anything to one another throughout the day. Christina and I sat in silence for what seemed to be an hour, just staring at Norman.

Once again that sinister little grin of his seemed more defined, like he was gratified in some way.

I was sitting at the computer and Christina was lying on the bed. In between moments of silence, one of us would randomly throw out a theory or two that didn't revolve around something supernatural. But we were only kidding ourselves. That fact became crystal clear in the moments ahead.

I had just turned around from my desk to talk to Christina again, who was still lying on the bed.

It was at that moment when we both reacted to a loud explosion outside. It was so extreme it shook the house. We were both stunned as we glanced at one another.

Immediately I thought car crash, dynamite, or a bomb of some sort.

Then the unspeakable happened. Within seconds of the sonic boom, I was hammered with what felt like a giant, one hundred pound bag of sand hitting me dead on.

Only there was no giant bag of sand.

I was struck with such great force the wind was completely taken out of me and I could not breathe. The impact, which was also caught on surveillance, knocked me off the chair in a very violent fashion.

This was no love tap. This was an intentional attack to floor me, and it did. It all happened so fast. I scrambled to grab anything to hold on to as I went down, even taking down with me a photography backdrop I was using for photo sessions with the grandkids.

Unseen force attacking me.

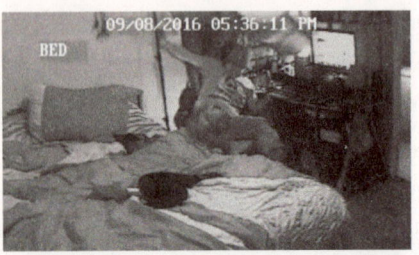
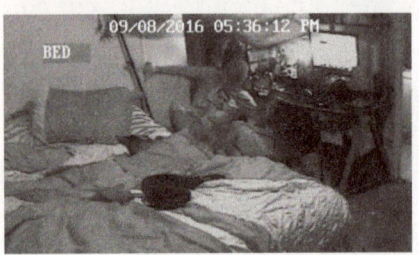

Falling to the floor.

The speed of the attack was uncanny. This all happened within a second.

I collected myself while Christina kept asking me if I was alright. She couldn't believe what she just witnessed. Christina even said there was no humanly possible way I could have made myself move like that.

She added that it was like I was shoved very violently by an invisible man.

I of course agreed. I can't say with certainty the loud sound and the attack were related. That part simply could be coincidence. But this was all going to the deep south way too fast. We were treading on dangerous ground now.

Even as I remember this while I type, my hands shake.

I sit here waiting to be grabbed or shoved or lifted unexpectedly.

When there is nothing there, and you can be bombarded with spiritual energy without warning at any time, living comfortably is never a luxury you have.

Nobody should ever have to live in fear, but we were. We thought we were in control and we thought we could end this at any moment.

But we couldn't. That is the most impotent feeling in the world.

You have to be prepared for extreme activity such as this, and typically I am. This wasn't the first time I had been attacked by an entity. But there was something different about this one. Our home was invaded. Our lives were being altered. It all pointed to a small toy that had very large ability.

All egos aside, something had to be done.

Happy birthday to me. My cat was dead and I had been physically attacked, again.

Enough was enough.

It was novel for research purposes to have a haunted doll in the home of two paranormal researchers, but once death enters the equation, it is time for the cause of death to exit.

A week had passed with very little excitement since I discovered the remains of Little F and put him to rest.

Nine

Looking back, I guess that's just how long it took Norman to contemplate his next move.

That day Christina was returning home from work when she noticed something sitting on the front porch. As she pulled in the driveway, the object wasn't clear enough to make out or even begin to describe.

She simply noticed something out of place on the porch, yet coincidentally placed perfectly so it would be noticed. Christina called me from her car as I was sitting at my desk.

First, she asked me if I had been outside at all that day and I told her no. Other than opening the door to let the dogs in and out, those were the only moments I had seen the outside world that day.

She said there was what looked like a rock sitting on the center of the porch in front of the door.

I did not recall seeing any rock at all that day, so I got up from my desk to meet Christina outside. I opened the front door and immediately saw it.

I started dancing around the porch like a maniac, drawing Christina's attention to hurry up and get out of the car.

As she was climbing out of the car I could hear her asking, "What is it?" in a panic over and over.

I picked the mysterious object up and placed it in my hand.

As Christina approached her eyes began to focus on what I was holding.

It was a skull.

But not just any skull.

It was Little F's skull.

There was no denying that this was done on purpose. Little F was physically dug up and his skull was placed on our front porch.

At first we couldn't say with certainty it was Little F, but we did know it was a small cat's skull.

It wasn't until we approached his grave and noticed it had been dug up that confirmation was made concerning the identity.

Dug up grave. Check.

Missing skull. Check.

Found skull. Check.

Once again I tried making a sandcastle out of water, but nothing stuck.

We learned a few things upon further examination. Our dogs did not do it. If they had, every bone in that grave would have been removed and scattered all over our property.

Never mind the fact that the skull had been so eloquently and conveniently placed. Sure, there was a chance that could happen perfectly at random, but I would have noticed it before now.

If one of the dogs had in fact dug it up, I would have seen it long before Christina, having let them in and out all day.

That left a maximum of two hours in between the time I let the dogs back in the house to the time Christina arrived home.

That meant that something had, in broad daylight, dug up Little F and placed his skull on the front porch for all the world to see. The ego this entity has goes right along with the know-it-all grin.

Our front porch surveillance caught nothing. The camera was angled to capture faces of visitors, not the floor of the porch.

Something very intelligent did this. It was too mastered to have been by chance. I still stood there, staring down at the skull in my hand.

Christina made a haunting point at that moment. She said, "How is it possible for Little F to have been completely decayed in only a week's time?"

I hadn't thought of that until she mentioned the idea. I was just so stunned and amazed at what I was holding in my hand I didn't stop to think beyond that. All rational thinking had flown out the window. The cat's remains should not have been so clean.

It wasn't like his body was lying out in the sun for every little critter to come take a nibble.

Little F had been buried under a shady tree. If anything it would have taken him three to five months or more to decay completely.

When you can't explain something by scientific means, you have no choice but to call it paranormal. So I added Little F's skull to our collection of haunted objects.

I was already at my wit's end with Norman and his games. It was like he was going out of his way to prove he could, not whether he should. He was laying claim to the role of Alpha.

It was well beyond time for us to take control.

10

Haunted Doll for Sale

At this point we were months into our experiences with Norman and waiting to see what the approaching hurricane was going to do.

If it were to hit us, it was predicted to be devastating with loss of power for days and inaccessible roads, so I wasted no time hitting the computer to sell Norman.

We certainly did not want to be stuck in the dark at the house for days with him still inside.

You may or may not know that allegedly haunted dolls go for extreme amounts of money to interested parties. I remember seeing one in particular advertised for $19,000.

The doll better be making me breakfast every morning for that price!

But I wasn't in the market for a novelty item. I was looking to get rid of our invited yet unwelcome guest.

I took to the internet and a popular auction site and created a personal page for Norman. I even included the video of the tests I conducted on him showing the ionic energy, the EMF reading, and the temperature drops.

I also included a written warning to interested parties that stated something to the effect:

I am not responsible for the actions of Norman, nor am I responsible for any paranormal activity that may occur once in your possession. Please be responsible and respect the subject at hand.

Within six hours of making his page public and offering him up for sale, thousands of people were inquiring about the doll.

I could not keep up with all of the questions coming through.

For me, it wasn't about the money. It was about getting him out of my house.

So at first he was advertised for an auction starting price of $50.

I figured that was a reasonable price for, if anything, an antique doll that's hard to find. I also thought that would make him move a little faster.

I was optimistic, considering all of the inquiries.

Then hundreds of people started to choose the option to "watch" the item—people who had a genuine interest in buying the item.

I told Christina with confidence that he was going to sell.

He was placed on a three-day auction.

On the day the auction was to end, Christina and I went out to dinner. She was questioning the auction, but I was still convinced he was going to sell, considering all of the watchers.

We returned home shortly after the auction ended, and I honestly expected to see him sold. But there was nothing. There was not a single bid on him.

I was shocked.

So I listed him for sale again, except this time I included a signed copy of my last book, *Dark Spirits: A Man Terrorized by the Supernatural*, in addition to lowering the auction starting price to $30.

Certainly that was going to make him more appealing, and I was so sure I had it right this time.

Up for sale he went again with one of my books for another three-day auction.

Like before, his page received thousands of views and hundreds of watchers.

More emails came flooding in with questions about the doll and the activity.

I started to tell people that I was planning on writing a novel that chronicled our experiences with him in the future. He would become even more valuable at that time.

The second auction went a little differently, and during this attempt I was finally seeing actual bids on Norman.

By the time the auction started closing in on the final hours, he was up to over 300 bids.

If that wasn't enough to convince me he was going to sell, I don't know what would.

Like before, something odd occurred. When the auction ended, there was no sale. The highest bidder did not win the auction. It was like he had never even been bid on at all.

According to this sale platform, if you bid, you are committed to make the purchase if you have the winning bid.

I immediately contacted the auction site about this issue or glitch in their programming, and still to this day have not received a response explaining how and why that happened.

They say the third time is a charm, so up for sale he went one last time. It was the same deal as before at the same price, including my book.

As you have probably guessed, there were thousands of views and hundreds of watchers and bidders.

But this time, he slipped through the cracks and sold! I was beginning to think my luck had changed. He sold to a young lady in Kentucky.

Once the payment went through, I quickly made the drive to the post office to rid my family of this burden and put an end to the awful toy story. We were relieved, to say the least, to finally have our home back to normal instead of consistently Norman.

A few weeks passed without incident until I received an email from the young girl who had purchased him. Apparently she never did receive the package. I returned to the post office to have them investigate.

As it turned out, the post office had no answer, but they did have Norman.

They could not explain why he was never shipped or, if he was, how he ended up back in their mail room. Even their tracking system brought up errors when attempting to find his whereabouts. I obtained the package and verified the address that was given to me, and it was accurate. So I once again paid for shipping and he was set to go.

I returned home and contacted the buyer with apologies and the lack of explanation I received from the post office. She was very understanding.

Weeks passed again without any trouble until I was contacted once more by the buyer. She did not receive Norman and the tracking was doing the same thing.

Every attempt we made to track him returned nothing but errors. This time I refunded the girl's money and returned to the post office. This time the package had been signed "return to sender."

As expected, the post office had no documentation or reason as to how or why.

I gave up.

Obviously Norman wasn't going to go anywhere willingly.

I returned home to see a disappointed look on my girlfriend's face when she saw me walk into the bedroom with the box.

She knew without me saying a word what was in it. A few choice words of profanity filled our bedroom.

What do we do now? To lighten the mood, I made a corny joke about how you can never kill the haunted dolls in the movies. No matter what you do, they always come back.

But this wasn't a movie and what we were dealing with was about to become much more serious. Norman was about to show us how much he disliked being discarded for a third time in his life. Bringing him back into the house opened the gates of hell with guns blazing.

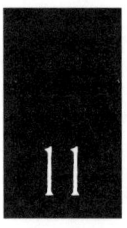

I Know

When your girlfriend's daughter comes running and screaming out of the house in nothing but a towel, you know something serious has just taken place. Hannah isn't one for theatrics, so when she's scared, it's authentic.

Shortly after all of the failed attempts at ridding our home of Norman, we decided to get outside for a while. We all needed some fresh air and time away from it, him, that, or whatever you want to call that thing. Christina and I decided to have a bonfire that evening.

We had a big fifty-gallon steel barrel outside that we frequently had fires in.

While the two of us were setting up the fire, Hannah said she was going to take a shower and then come out to join us.

About twenty minutes had passed when completely out of nowhere Hannah comes flying out the front door screaming at the top of her lungs, claiming somebody was in her bathroom.

Still dripping wet from the shower, she claimed to have seen a shadow through the shower curtain near the sink. When she turned the shower off to look, she noticed a few words written on the mirror.

Knowing I only had a small window of time before the condensation on the mirror dissipated, I quickly ran into the house and grabbed a camera to document it.

When I got to her bathroom I was taken aback by the words "I Know" written very large in the foggy mirror.

The words appeared to be written with a greasy finger, like a finger of someone who just ate chicken wings or something.

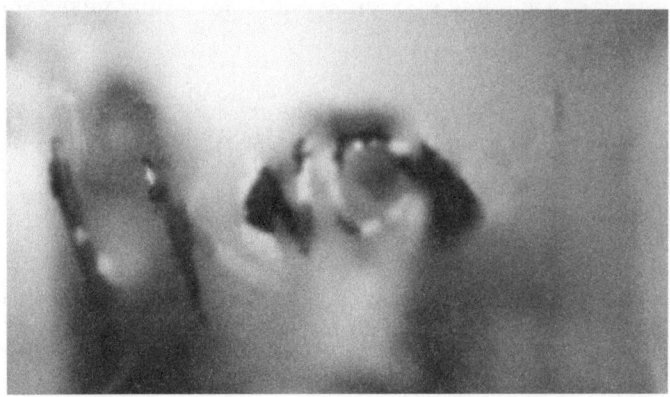

"I know" written on the mirror.

I took a handful of pictures before it faded completely.

I started reviewing them immediately in the window of the digital camera.

I fell back against the wall when I noticed Norman's face in the mirror. I didn't notice him at first because my eyes were attempting to focus on the words in the mirror. But once I looked again, his face stood right out to me.

I had to stop and digest all of this.

How was this even remotely possible? Yet there he was as plain as day standing behind me.

To put things in perspective for you, you can see my eye in the "O."

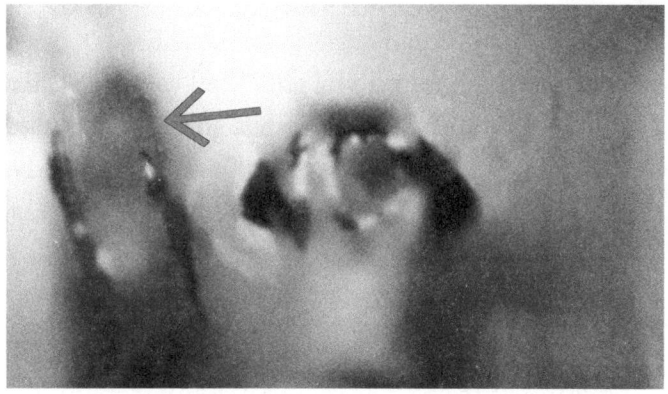

Norman behind the words.

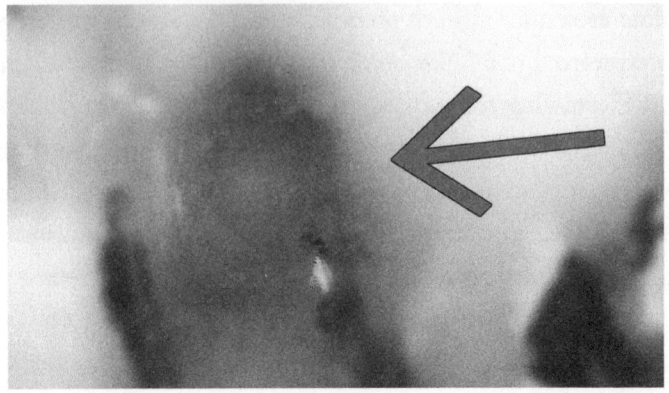

Norman's face in mirror.

Christina joined me while Hannah waited outside, refusing to enter. She too noticed the greasy letters. You could still see the words if you looked at the mirror from a certain angle.

"I know" is such a common phrase that often shows up during paranormal research. It's cliché and a bit corny at this point, considering how much it has been used in horror films and novels, including my own works, but how else do you say it?

I have to share this case as it happens. This time it really hit home. If you know something, you simply say *I know*. When you break it down, there are many other words commonly found during paranormal investigating, such as names, labels like "mom" and "dad," and simple yes and no responses.

So I guess it simply is what it is.

As we searched through the house to make sure we didn't have an actual living, breathing intruder, I kept thinking about how the message discovered on the mirror was to be interpreted.

Having learned of Christina's tragic past that mimicked Norman's dismal history, I couldn't help but wonder if that was what he meant. Did he know that Christina lost her son and only her daughter survived?

This made me ponder the idea that maybe Norman was looking for surrogates. My girlfriend and her daughter were to take the place of his lost mother and estranged sister. To me, this seemed logical considering everything that had-happened so far and the uncanny similarities in the stories.

There was just too much to call it coincidence. This would also explain why I seemed to be the target of the violent outbursts while the women of the house and even guests were never harmed.

There was no father in Norman's life or his sister's, which means there would be no need for me if he was attempting to recreate what he once watched through plastic eyes.

From the protection statue being thrown at my head, the disturbing voices calling my name, Norman always returning to the house, the grisly murder of my cat, and the physical attack, all pointed to wanting me out of the picture. But it didn't end there.

We returned outside to the fire to collect ourselves, calm Hannah down, and try to talk through this as a family.

Any way you slice it, finding something written on the mirror after you shower is disturbing. Whether it is paranormal or not, somebody or something was in the house and did it. That to me is the most frightening part.

I could see the fear in Hannah's eyes. Here stood a fifteen-year-old girl who was alone in the house simply taking a shower, only to discover somebody had been in her bathroom.

I stood close to the barrel fire while Christina was consoling Hannah about fifteen feet away on the other side of her car.

I was just about to put some more wood in the barrel when our peaceful moment was shattered by the sound of a gunshot.

The shot came from within the barrel and was only a foot or so from my hand.

I immediately jumped back while Christina was yelling at me to get away from the barrel.

As I was quickly running toward them behind the car, more shots were fired. One right after another.

I counted at least eight separate shots as sparks flew from inside the barrel.

Shortly after the sequence of blasts, things calmed down and I slowly walked back over to the fire.

Nothing else happened at that moment, but we all were a bit on edge. It was best for us to go back inside together.

We collected ourselves in the master bedroom. All taking turns glancing between the monitor controlling the surveillance cameras and Norman.

I reassured them that the barrel was always cleaned out prior to starting a new fire. The ash is removed and a new fire begins.

I was convinced, however, that somebody had placed live ammunition in the barrel as a trap.

During our conversation, Hannah grabbed our attention as she was viewing the surveillance. She said she just sat there and watched her bedroom door open by itself.

If you knew how I had her bedroom door rigged, you would be just as dumbfounded as we were. I should tell you also that it had never done that before.

With four dogs always wanting to break into your room when you aren't there, I rigged up a simple latch on her door to prevent them from doing that.

Without the latch, a firm push would cause the door to open.

With the latch, it could not be opened. I quickly found the part on the surveillance footage where she claimed it started opening.

Sure enough, the three of us sat there and watched her door unlatch and then open slowly to reveal the darkness of her room.

I wish I could say it all ended there for Hannah, but sadly it did not.

Hannah's exterior bedroom door latch.

Well after we had all went to bed, Norman decided to continue his maniacal pestering.

Two in the morning brought with it an awakening that rattled the house.

Hannah was screaming at the top of her lungs. You could tell she was screaming through tears, yelling "mom" as loud as she could.

Christina and I nearly fell out of bed, and all the dogs jumped up barking. For a second, our bedroom was total chaos. We bolted out the bedroom door and ran into the living room.

Latch in closed position.

In the living room stood Hannah in tears and nearly hyperventilating. She told us that something pulling on her blankets woke her up.

When explaining to us what had transpired, Hannah said at the time she remained quiet for a moment, thinking she must have been dreaming. She just continued to be still in the bed.

But then she felt pressure, like somebody had just sat down near her feet.

Suddenly she could feel something crawling up the bed. She said it felt human. Hannah described it as a person crawling on their hands and knees on top of her.

It was at that moment in time she panicked and decided to sit up, but she was unable to.

Immediately her body suffered from a paralysis. Hannah told us it felt just like a person had crawled up on top of her and was refusing to let her move.

She struggled and struggled until it let go and she was able to break free and scream. She immediately jumped from her bed and ran out into the living room to meet us.

Having shared in a similar experience as a child, I knew damn well what happened to her was spiritual in nature and potentially savage.

Christina and I of course inspected her room. There was no sign of an intruder. Attacking Hannah was the icing on the cake. She had been a victim all evening. It was an exciting night to say the least. Christina and I decided that with Hannah being the target of a handful of separate paranormal incidences happening so closely together, we needed to get her out.

She packed a bag and we took her over to her brother Matthew's house to stay until we could figure all of this out.

The next morning I went out to the now-extinguished fire barrel to examine the ash. I sifted through the ash, hoping to snag something that would explain what caused the sparks and the sound of gunshots the night prior.

I found three empty shell cases from a .22 caliber bullet.

That was all I needed to see. I didn't need to locate the five others to know they were placed in there purposely to cause one of us harm.

We own firearms, and a .22 rifle is one of them. Those bullets came from our bedroom, where they were locked up in a cabinet.

Apparently somebody had found the key and was well educated enough to be methodical knowing exactly what they would do under extreme heat.

But we had bigger problems on the way. We were about to find ourselves trapped and isolated between the horror inside and the horror outside from an approaching storm.

12

Hurricane Matthew

The coincidences with Matty, Matthew, and Hurricane Matthew during our time with Norman was just unbelievable.

Matty was the doll's original name. Matthew was Christina's oldest son, and Hurricane Matthew was about to deliver its own brand of destruction.

Even the radar image of Hurricane Matthew looked evil and menacing.

The hurricane appeared like a giant skull eating away at the earth.

I remember when images of the hurricane resembling a skull took the internet by...well, storm.

It was almost as if in that moment the whole world was experiencing something paranormal.

Norman cannot take claim to that hurricane. I would be a damn arrogant fool to state otherwise and claim a doll actually manifested a severe storm.

But the timing could not have been better. October became scary real quick, and it wasn't because of Halloween.

For those of us who live in the South, we are just as prepared for hurricanes as the North is prepared for blizzards. Weather in North Carolina is a nationwide joke. It can be twenty-two degrees one day and seventy-seven degrees the next.

North Carolina weather is beyond paranormal. But certain extreme weather delivers better opportunities to experience the supernatural. And more paranormal occurrences were definitely in our forecast.

Storms bring ionic energy with them, and to save you pages of explanation, that will sum up the relevance to the paranormal.

Air molecules are constantly breaking apart at great lengths from sunlight, wind, moving water, and even radiation. The end results in an abundance of negative ions.

But don't let that word *negative* fool you. In this case, it is a good thing. Negative ions actually make you feel good. You would think just the opposite, but positive ions actually harm us.

We are surrounded by positive ions every day from electromagnetic fields (EMF) generated from electrical devices and atmospheric changes.

You would be surprised how much of your everyday life is affected by ionic energy. Extreme amounts can impair the brain and your thought process. Your immune system can suffer greatly, causing anxiety, fatigue, vertigo, nausea, hallucinations, and difficulty breathing.

To put it bluntly, before, during, and after a storm, you are exposed to approximately 3,250 positive and negative ions per cubic centimeter.

So you can only imagine what a severe storm does to bring that number up.

Positive ions bad. Negative ions good.

With me so far? Why is this relevant?

Paranormal research focuses a great deal on the impact of electromagnetic fields and ionic energy, not only to the human body and psyche, but to the spiritual realm as well.

It is almost unanimously agreed upon among researchers that higher amounts of EMF and ionic energy can promote more defined paranormal activity.

In other words, the more those types of energies are present, the more capable a spirit can become. They could possibly now move objects, speak, manifest, and make physical contact.

The stronger the field, the stronger the ghost. Therefore, storms are a good thing when it comes to researching the paranormal.

Again, I'm a psyche guy, not a physicist, so continue your own research on that if you wish.

A spirit is no different than a human being when it comes down to energy. We must eat to gain strength and to ultimately survive.

A spirit must absorb energy to gain strength. The more energy that is readily available, the more physical ability a spirit will have.

We were about to be sitting right in the middle of a smorgasbord for ghosts.

There would be nowhere for us to go outside or even the means to do so.

Most hauntings are subtle, lacking the available energy to feed off of. Everyday household items produce EMFs and other energies that spirits can, will, and do use with minimal occurrence.

Norman could already perform amazing feats without the help of a severe storm. Thoughts were racing as I contemplated what Norman would do if given the opportunity. Hurricane Matthew was approaching and we had a lot to prepare for.

Our home was only about forty-five miles from the shoreline, and our area was under severe warning with a direct hit in the forecast.

Aside from needing the normal bread and milk and essential supplies, we also had to be prepared for what this storm could do to Norman. Talk about being stuck between a rock and a hard place.

The first half of our preparation went easy. A quick run into town to the grocery store gave us everything we needed to survive physically. The second half of our preparation was a bit more extensive.

Even during a midgrade thunderstorm, we tend to lose power. Which means we lose water and everything in the fridge.

We live about five miles out of town and with the exception of a few neighbors, we weren't exactly on the electric company's priority list.

A normal storm could put us into apocalyptic living for two to three days.

This was going to be a full-blown hurricane.

There was going to be an abundance of flooding, fallen trees, dangerously high winds, and debris flying everywhere.

However, Christina and I were more concerned about the electrical blackouts and a sixteen-inch mischievous, loathsome doll creeping around the house.

We would be without the surveillance once the hurricane hit. There was no question about that. We charged up every portable infrared and night vision camera we had in addition to a handful of spare batteries. Every flashlight and camera light was freshly charged and prepared. Every piece of equipment we had for paranormal research was locked and loaded with enough batteries to last us for weeks.

If all of that failed us, we had an entire box full of candles.

If we were pushed to desperation, we could recharge certain pieces of equipment with a car charger. So I would say we were ready.

We locked up every door into the house and waited as Hurricane Matthew approached.

While we still had power, we kept a close eye on the Doppler radar both on the television and on the internet. We were going to know the exact moment Matthew was going to hit.

As expected, within just a few hours, Matthew's outer bands hit our area and the power went out and all of our equipment went on.

It was about nine in the evening when this happened, and because of all the chaos outside, it was hard to determine what was coming from where.

Banging was a constant. The wind was atrocious. The entire house was shaking.

It was difficult to say whether anything audible was paranormal or the storm. We were going to have to experience visual activity to be sold on anything. So Christina and I decided to place Norman in a neutral location. We put him on the kitchen table in an upright position. Of course we placed a camera on him, set to record any motion if by chance he moved.

Christina went back to the master bedroom and I went to sit in Hannah's room. The rain was coming down so hard that we needed to use radios to communicate even though we were only fifty feet from one another.

After about an hour, my ears started to adjust to the sounds outside from the storm. It was easier for me to determine what was coming from outside and what was coming from inside.

Christina called me on the radio to ask if I was hearing music. I told her I wasn't hearing anything but the pounding rain and debris hitting the house.

But she was hearing music. It wasn't a melody, though. It sounded more like drumming. At first, I thought it was just water rhythmically hitting a bucket or something outside, but to go on for over five minutes in perfect time…I had to rule that idea out.

All of the dogs were with Christina in the bedroom while we were separated. We had to consider their movement as well, so we made sure to be very aware of their location at all times.

We had equipped our dog Tank with a vest and night vision head camera set to constantly record. So whenever he walked through the house, whatever he saw, we would later see while reviewing the footage.

Tank geared up for investigating.

It's pretty neat seeing the world through a dog's eyes, even if sometimes that world is a dark one.

Tank is used to this. He often accompanies us on cases, so I had designed a special camera rig just for him.

A few moments had passed since we had reviewed what I dubbed as drumming.

Come to think of it, that makes me think of the little drummer boy. That didn't hit me until writing this.

Yet another reference to Christmas.

I returned to Hannah's bedroom and Christina remained in the master bedroom.

A few hours passed without incident, but then Christina once again reached out to me on the radio.

She asked if I had just walked through the living room. Now where I was sitting in Hannah's room, I couldn't see through the door to the living room. But from where she was sitting in the master bedroom, she could.

I told her I had not moved.

She said she swore that she had seen a dark figure walk through the living room and into the kitchen. She naturally assumed it was me.

I told her to come over to my location so I could see the footage on her camera. She did and I looked. Sure enough, it appeared as if something solid black and about five feet or so tall walked through the living room.

I watched it over and over, thinking maybe somebody was crazy and was out driving around and their car lights threw some shadows around. That was not the case.

But why a five-foot figure?

Could this go back to the theory that the spirit inside of Norman had aged and was now an older man?

Was he out of Norman now? Was the ionic energy from the storm bringing all of this out? It made sense to me, and I even said so to Christina.

As we were discussing the shadowy figure, Christina stopped midsentence to ask where the dogs were at?

The dogs were always within view or directly with one of us.

We both crept slowly to the doorway to see out into the living room. There stood Tank staring into the kitchen with his tail fully erect. He was on to something. That was the direction the shadowy figure went, and that was also where Norman was. None of the other dogs were in sight.

We could only assume they stayed in the master bedroom.

Then, without warning, both Christina and I jumped when Tank started barking.

Let me tell you something about his bark: it rattles windows, it about gives me a heart attack when I'm sleeping, and he barks at anything that moves.

If a leaf falls from a tree outside, Tank lets us know.

We stood there watching Tank's body language as he stood poised, throwing out bark after bark.

I finally whispered to Christina that we should creep up and see what he was barking at.

There was a back door to the kitchen, as well as a window, and maybe he was seeing something not so paranormal.

It's not uncommon during disasters for would-be thieves to take advantage of people. So we were going to check.

We made our way through the living room as quietly as possible. It wasn't hard. The outside elements masked our movement really well.

Tank didn't even hear us coming.

But before we could get to him, he started a very slow and cautious walk backward from the kitchen entrance where he once stood barking.

While our attention was on Tank as he nervously walked backward, a loud boom caused me to gasp, Christina screamed, and Tank darted off with his tail between his legs.

He shot directly for the master bedroom where the other dogs remained. Guess he was thinking safety in numbers.

But, like I've said before, Tank is a tank. He's a force to be reckoned with. He is only two years old and well over one hundred pounds. And since Norman was brought into the house, he has become very timid and jumpy. I refer to him as my gentle giant now.

Now we had to investigate what in the world made that loud boom in the kitchen.

After rushing into the kitchen, both of us just stopped and looked at each other and said, "No way."

Norman was now lying on the floor.

Now you have to remember he was sitting upright in the middle of the kitchen table.

It would have taken some intervening and some force to make him move all the way across the table to fall off.

Tank knew something wasn't right.

Our first instinct was to check the camera that was trained on Norman.

Unfortunately, and I'm embarrassed to mention this, the battery on the camera was dead.

It had been so long into the night that we had completely forgotten to check the camera and change out the battery.

We had nothing to show for it, other than our perspective with our own cameras while walking into the kitchen and discovering him on the floor.

Of course there was Tank's odd behavior to couple with that as well. But there still was nothing to show. It would all be hearsay.

Then it hit me.

Tank's night vision head camera had been running this whole time. That device is awesome. It will record for up to six hours in total blackout in high definition. We grabbed Norman and brought him back with us into the master bedroom. The three of us went in, all the dogs went out. They did not want to be around that doll.

I have always been a firm believer that animals can sense things we cannot, so I wasn't going to question for a second their reasoning for vacating the room.

I tried to call Tank into the room, but he refused to enter. He just stood in the living room staring at me, barking away. I can only imagine what he was trying to say.

Unfortunately, with Tank's camera, we needed the computer to see his footage. There wasn't a display on his camera, unlike the rest of ours, to review previously recorded material. I was a bit upset at that, but eventually we would have power again.

Christina and I quickly changed out the batteries in our cameras in case anything else happened, and then we discussed what to do with Norman next.

Honestly, I wanted to throw his ass outside and let Matthew meet Matty and wash him away into the darkness. It was just a thought.

I suggested we put him in the living room on the couch where we had a direct line of sight from the bedroom. By doing so, we could just sit with cameras aimed and watch him.

Christina agreed.

The three of us went into the living room, the dogs went back into the bedroom.

The more I think about the dogs' behavior, the more I believe their anxiety level must have been over the top.

When you are a dog owner, you know your animals' mannerisms and characteristics. Seeing all of our best friends' heads down and cowering was a bit depressing. I almost felt like it was our fault.

But at the same time, maybe the chaos outside was making them wary and Norman had nothing to do with it.

That thought quickly went out the window about as fast as a road sign that had just hit the side of the house.

That's right. After a loud smack on the living room wall, we shined our lights out through the windows to see a road sign lying there.

The wind was absolutely merciless.

The 121 mile an hour wind was no joke.

To put that in perspective, it is impossible to walk in eighty miles an hour wind, let alone 121. Flying objects at that speed become lethal. That road sign could have taken a person's head off. One hundred twenty-one miles an hour wind could lift an average person off the ground. Wind that speed has a drag force of hundreds and hundreds of pounds.

The road sign was for a one-way street.

I couldn't even tell you where the closest one-way street is around here. Who knows how far that sign traveled.

However, the excitement was far from over, and we were about to get yet another amazing visual recording.

The two of us went back to our spot in the bedroom and focused once again on the living room where Norman sat like a good little boy on the couch.

As if most of what you read so far wasn't the most unbelievable material, I can't lie.

Christina and I were sitting on the bed in silence, watching the living room with our cameras documenting everything.

All of the dogs were lined up beside us along the bed.

You want to talk about nearly soiling yourself? To my left I heard the most vivid breath. It felt like it was right over my shoulder. No question the drawn-out exhale came from a man.

I turned around as quickly as I could to capture what ended up being a better look at our mysterious shadow figure from earlier.

Except this time, he was in the mirror. The most haunting part about this was him not only gaining my attention, but the fact you can clearly see there is nobody standing in front of that mirror.

That extremely threatening and intimidating looking entity was in the mirror. He was like a reflection without the image to reflect.

His lifeless eyes housed a thousand stories that all seemed to be told at once as I sat completely frozen in fear.

You would have to see it to believe it, but luckily you can.

All my life, searching for these experiences. All my life, waiting for the undeniable truth of intelligent existence beyond our human life. And it all fell within my own family's haunting.

The entity is revealed.

There it is. There's the proof.

In a snap of a finger he vanished.

The door to our bedroom slammed shut. It slammed so hard books from the shelf fell off, and other objects we couldn't even see, only hear, hit the floor. All of the dogs immediately ran into our master bathroom.

Christina and I sat there in awe at what we witnessed.

What was that black entity? Was he what Norman was holding inside? Did this storm fuel him enough to show his true self?

If that were the case, and I think it was, I definitely did not want to see it again, nor did I have any intention of ever bringing it out of Norman. It could stay right there.

A quick review of our cameras showed we had indeed captured the door slamming shut.

I was petrified.

The two of us sat in shock, awe, and confusion staring at the door.

Tank came out of the bathroom and very cautiously started sniffing around the door before returning to the bathroom with the rest of the dogs.

Shortly after that we started to hear a series of booms and smacks coming from behind the door.

The lights in both the master bedroom and bathroom started flickering off and on.

This was impossible. If the electricity was truly trying to come back on, other devices would have been powering up as well.

Instead it was just the lights.

It was at that moment that one of the most incredible and frightening things took place.

The entire bedroom door was ripped from its hinges in an extremely violent fashion and thrown full force into the living room.

And our cameras caught it.

Door flying off its hinges.

For as much as we both had witnessed over the years with violent haunts, this was getting out of control.

Door completely ripped its from frame.

A door had just been physically ripped from the hinges and thrown into the living room like it was weightless.

What do you say to something like that?

I jumped up from the bed and slowly made my way into the living room to film the now-destroyed door.

Norman just sat in his same spot smirking away at me.

As I shined my flashlight around the room, I instantly noticed interior damage to the living room.

No windows were shattered. The front door that led to the living room was fine, other than the large amount of water that was seeping in from underneath.

With urgency, I called for Christina to come see what I was seeing.

When she entered the room, her jaw dropped as I shined my flashlight on each and every hole in the wall. These holes were the size of a fist.

It was as if somebody lost their temper and started punching the wall.

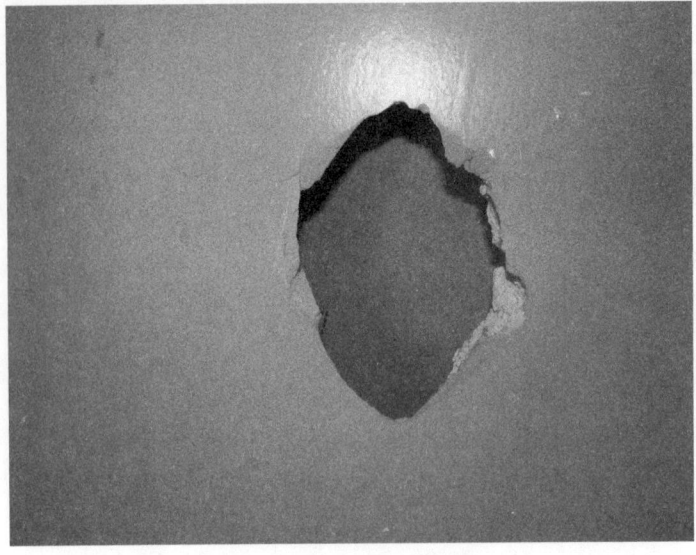

One of the holes in the wall.

We also noticed family portraits had been knocked from the wall. Glass was shattered everywhere.

I cleaned up the glass so the dogs wouldn't walk through it. I just kept shaking my head and saying to Christina how insane this all was.

Exterior damage I get. But interior damage without a breach was impossible, unless somebody else was in the house.

The only other…thing in the house was Norman.

After all of the heart pounding excitement, the morning was upon us.

Wall cracking open.

It was still dreary out, but most of Matthew's rain and wreckage had passed.

Our front yard was no longer a yard. It was a pond. We couldn't even see the road out front. Trees were down as far as we could see, and trash was everywhere.

From just our view, it was a total disaster.

A few days passed before we were able to leave the house. The activity from Norman seemed to have ceased for the time being.

We had a truck and wanted to get out and about just in case people needed help.

But before doing that, now that we had power, we needed to take a quick look through Tank's eyes.

I loaded the footage from his head camera into the computer and Christina and I sat glued to the monitor.

During the time Tank was standing at the kitchen entrance barking, we could vividly see Norman sitting on the table where we left him.

As Tank started to back out slowly, right as he started to turn toward the master bedroom, Norman hit the floor. Which now let us know what set Tank running.

The clip of video was so fast and so short, his camera didn't actually capture anything from the table.

Since his head was turning, all he captured was Norman in the air before he hit the floor.

Hurricane Matthew 161

Norman jumping from the table.

At least Tank's camera was able to validate that something caused Norman to fall from that table, or he did it himself.

Regardless, it's hard to say either way. Maybe this was a frame of Norman walking or running or even jumping.

We just don't know. Either way, the image is haunting.

Shortly after reviewing the rest of Tank's footage, we took the truck out to drive around town to see just how bad the destruction was. It was awful.

Entire roads were completely washed away. Lost dogs were everywhere. Even the town itself still had no power. All of the fast food restaurants, all of the grocery stores, and every business in town could not operate. Without power, it was a dead zone.

People were suggesting that neighboring towns had power and supplies, so we risked a drive to find one. Detour after detour brought us to a store about thirty minutes from home.

I couldn't believe what I was seeing when we walked in.

All of the shelves were bare, and this was a major, well-known store. All of their food, batteries, and other useful supplies had been cleaned out. I saw workers loading up truckloads of food that went bad due to the power outages.

It truly was like Armageddon had taken place.

So we drove a little farther west to find a store to replenish the necessities we lost during the storm.

A few days later, the power was back, but the area still looked like a war zone.

Every road had large piles of debris plowed to the sides. Houses were missing their roofs. Vehicles were under four to five feet of water.

It was a depressing situation to see.

To make matters worse, the water was only going to be getting higher from the lakes and streams as it traveled back toward us from the north. The town wasn't going to be itself for quite some time.

Children didn't go to school for weeks because there was no safe way to get there.

It was dreadful.

Following the hurricane, the next month or so was fairly quiet. But that's only because we were rarely home. Hurricane Matthew acted like the calm before the even bigger storm.

Thanksgiving came and went without a hitch. Norman was lifeless.

We were quite busy working out contracts with clients on new and old cases, so we were hit-and-miss at home. It wasn't anything for us to be gone three to four days at a time.

Hannah continued to stay with her brother while we traveled, hoping to have all of our other investigative work finished before the Christmas holiday.

Anytime we arrived home, I spent time reviewing the surveillance, but nothing was ever out of the ordinary.

The anniversary of Norman's fire was rapidly approaching, and we were waiting in anticipation.

13

December Chills

Christmas was two weeks away and I found myself home and alone once more.

Considering there had been very little interaction with Norman since the hurricane, I decided I was going to attempt to bring him out.

Other than my initial tests with the doll and our luck with the surveillance, we had very little concrete evidence in support of Norman's existence.

Sure, we had plenty of personal experiences and I certainly said the surveillance footage was the end-all to any questions regarding validity.

But one thing that had really yet to be explored fully was a communication session. A purposeful attempt to communicate with what hid inside of Norman is what I set out to do. After witnessing myself the darkness from within Norman standing beside us in that mirror, I desired to know more. However, I did not want to antagonize too much. I can't lie, the sight of that shadow figure was permanently engraved on my brain. I have seen them before, in the past, but never with such melancholy and emotionless presence attached and certainly not in the comforts of my own home.

I figured no time was better than the present, since it had been weeks without interaction and I was alone. Being alone meant I could immediately rule out any outside interference from other people. If something happened in the house, it would either have been done by me, Norman, or one of the dogs, all of which would be documented.

I took my laptop and placed it on the kitchen table with the on-board camera recording. That camera covered the kitchen, the living room, a small stand with an old lamp, and a room we just used for junk.

After spending a little time digging through Christina's jewelry box, I found a large gold Christian cross on a necklace. I figured if whatever entity resided in my house was in fact evil by religious definition, they might not have been too keen on seeing a cross.

I also thought I would experiment a little more with electromagnetic field testers. Not only would this help me monitor any fluctuations in electromagnetic fields, but it would also validate that an energy field was moving.

Armed with a cross, camera, and EMF detector, I sat down at the dining room table to attempt communication with the entity. It was one in the afternoon.

I placed the cross at the edge of the table alongside the EMF detector. With the laptop camera rolling, I started to speak.

"Is there anybody with me right now?" I asked.

Instantly, I heard a faint scratching sound come from Hannah's bedroom. Her door was wide open, so I could easily hear if anything moved around in there. I leaned over in my chair to where I could see into the bedroom.

I asked if the spirit was the one making the scratching sound and if they could do it again.

Right on cue, the scratching sound occurred one more time. This time, however, the sound was much louder, like somebody dragging their fingernails down a wall.

I was a bit creeped out. I was not feeling anything positive. Knowing at this point that I was speaking to a spirit, or more fitting, Norman, I asked it to come closer to the kitchen table.

I pointed out the EMF meter and explained that the closer they came, the higher the number would go and the faster the lights would flash. This would tell me the spirit was right beside me.

I asked to be approached, and the EMF lit up with an explosion of light. The lights were flashing extremely rapidly and the needle on the meter was buried past the highest level allotted for that device.

I then picked up the gold cross and dangled it in front of the table. The EMF meter immediately dropped back down to zero like nothing was there. I placed the cross back on the table and the meter maxed out again.

I went back and forth with this routine. I would move the cross off the table, and then I would put it back. Each and every time the meter would stop and start just like it did the first time.

It was evident at this point the entity was not very fond of that cross. It was also terrifying to realize that the spirit had that much energy. The readings I was documenting are not very common. This is especially true in an area that is nearly empty of electronic devices.

Was I to now start thinking in terms of religion or was that all simply coincidence?

Who are we to even begin to think we know the intentions of a spirit? The cross could mean nothing, or it could mean everything, but for now, all I could go by was what could be seen and heard.

With that in mind, I asked the entity if they were angry at me living there. Immediately, Hannah's bedroom door shut and latched. The atmosphere around me became very still.

I stood up and walked over to the bedroom door and reopened it. I then sat back down at the table. I apparently had struck a nerve with my line of questioning.

Proceeding with a line of communication, I asked if the entity wished for me to leave, and without hesitation a metallic scraping sound shot out of the master bedroom.

It sounded like somebody dragging a metal bucket.

I leaned over in my chair again to view the master bedroom. What happened next about gave me a heart attack. I started to stand up. My intentions were to walk back over to my bedroom door. I took one step in that direction when the loudest, most disturbing animalistic hiss caught me by such surprise that I literally stumbled backward into the wall and smacked my hand against my chest.

My heart was pounding out of my chest. I stood there clenching my chest and composing myself. I simply said out loud that it was fine and that I would sit back down. I did.

At that moment, beyond a shadow of a doubt, I knew that whatever was in my house was more than just your average spirit. This entity was very dark, angry, strong, and not afraid to intimidate. Believe me when I say it was intimidating.

I sat at the table in silence for a few minutes before starting my line of questioning again.

One more time I prompted the spirit to approach the table, and just like before the EMF detector gave me a light show.

Knowing that I had to take this further for my own peace of mind, I decided to test the spirit's tolerance. The entity obviously did not like the fact we were sharing the home, so I used that to fuel the uncanny events that happened next.

I decided to make a simple statement.

In a confident and stern fashion, I told the spirit that this was my house and we play by my rules.

I was barely finished with that sentence when the old lamp on the little stand directly to my right powered on and shook and flickered sporadically like a malfunctioning strobe light at a disco.

Of course, I jerked quickly to look in that direction, nearly separating my head from my neck.

I sat there dumbfounded. Apparently the entity did not appreciate my choice of words.

I leaned back in my chair and started to breathe in and out very slowly. This was a lot to take in. The activity in my home was very abundant and more than I had seen at a location in many years. It reminded me all too well of darker times and past investigations that led to malevolent behavior and colleagues getting hurt.

While I was sitting still in the chair, the air surrounding me became bitter cold. The temperature drop was undoubtedly noticeable, and it sent shivers down my spine.

I would later discover that the cold temperature was accompanied by something else.

Now I do have to clarify a personal feeling.

You know, it is one thing to witness spiritual activity firsthand and in real time. It is another for something to be happening and not have a clue it's even going on.

When you later learn that something was right there, so close, and you were oblivious to it—well, my friends, that is the scariest feeling of them all.

It is downright unsettling. I later discovered on the camera footage recording on the laptop that supernatural activity was literally occurring directly behind me.

After the excitement of the lamp situation, I decided to take a break and review everything that had been documented by my video camera.

I started the video over and began watching my entire communication session. Where I was sitting, in the recording, you can see the junk room door as I stated before.

I was staring off into the living room when that door cracked open ever so slightly. It continued to open at such a remarkably slow and patient pace that watching the video literally gave me cold chills.

This was incredible to realize. To turn a doorknob and push open a door requires force. I was left speechless realizing the amount of strength and energy this spirit must control.

This happened right behind me while experiencing the extreme temperature drop.

As I watched the footage over and over, I kept feeling as if something was in the darkness of that room, peering out and staring right through me.

I certainly can't validate that, but that was the feeling I had.

I watched the video a few more times before closing the laptop to collect myself.

I was feeling very exhausted, dizzy, empty, and a little disoriented as I sat in silence at the kitchen table.

My communication session lasted about an hour and a half. That was a lot of great footage and experiences to have gained and documented in such a short amount of time.

However, Norman wanted to make sure he had the last word.

As I was sitting at the table, the silence in the house was broken by the sound of pure white noise at full volume. I jumped out of the chair and ran toward the source of the noise.

The sound was bouncing all over the house. I should have been surprised, but I wasn't when I discovered the sound was coming from a television in the master bedroom.

Right before I entered the room, the television turned off and the sound ceased. The ear-bursting white noise sounded like somebody saying "shhh" infinitely. I looked over at Norman and asked myself "how is that even possible?" I took it a step further and even answered myself by saying aloud, "It's not."

A few hours later, Christina arrived home to find me listening to the television with one of her stethoscopes. I'm sure it was a sight for her. She didn't even bother asking.

She stopped, looked at me, then made her way to the bathroom for a shower.

In retrospect, the use of a stethoscope to hear the internal timbre of the television was quite symbolic considering what happened next.

14

Heart Still Beating

It has been a common belief among paranormal researchers that spirits, ghosts, demons—or whatever you want to call them—can, do, and will kill.

There has been story after story after story about people dying by the incorporeal hand of an entity.

Heart attacks have been to blame and seem to be more common than you would think. "Scared to death" seems to be a real thing. Are malevolent ghosts really scaring someone to death or are they literally judge, jury, and executioner?

I have personally handled cases that involved such phenomena, but I never once thought that something like that would happen to me. The only difference is I survived and I consider myself to be very lucky.

You can read in my other books about the cases I worked where certain haunted rooms actually caused heart attacks in the guests. It truly is frightening to think this is possible.

But for me, the signs were there—just not the signs you would commonly relate to having a heart attack.

The 911 calls. That whole ordeal changed perspective the day I almost died and had to call that number to save my life.

Was Norman attempting to tell me something back when all of those phantom calls were being made to emergency services?

As I mentioned earlier, if you consider the backstory, there was never a father figure in Norman's life.

The doll didn't have a father, but from what I have seen, I do believe the soul trapped inside that doll is the soul of the twin brother who was never born. Norman wanted things the way he was used to. He just wanted a mother and his friend in the form of a twin sister.

In our case, he just wanted Christina and Hannah, and he was doing everything in his power to get that message across to me. From objects being thrown at me to bullets flying in all directions, Norman was making it very clear he wanted me to vacate his new home.

But this time, on this day, he took it to the extreme.

As if being shot at by bullets in a burning barrel wasn't extreme enough, he had to beat me from the inside out. His warnings and his attempts to rid the home of me had failed.

We were just a little over a week away from Christmas and I was home alone working on the manuscript for this book. Hannah was at school and Christina was at work. I was working on the chapter you just read when I started to become extremely dizzy.

I stood up from my desk and walked into the kitchen for a glass of water, thinking that maybe dehydration was the reason for the light-headed feeling. It was truly overwhelming.

It was as if I had been spinning around in circles as fast as I could for minutes and then suddenly stopped. All inanimate objects seemed to be alive. Everything around me was moving, which made it very difficult to walk.

I managed to make my way back into the bedroom and back to my desk to collect myself. At that moment I stared at Norman and his "I just did something" grin.

I couldn't shake the dizziness. It was really starting to bring out severe anxiety in me.

As I sat there, I could feel my heart beating faster and harder. I could feel it in my skull and all throughout my body.

Nothing like this had ever happened to me before. This was new. This was scary.

Thirty-nine years old and my heart was running a marathon I didn't sign up for. My head began to nod downward repeatedly without warning as I sat in my chair as if I was about to black out.

I stood up and threw myself on the bed thinking that maybe if I was lying down, whatever was going on would relax.

That was not the case. The symptoms progressed.

I made my way to the phone in an attempt to call Christina to get her advice on what was going on with my body. I called three or four times and every time the lady who answered the phone would place me on hold and never retrieve Christina. I would hang up and try again. But I never was able to actually get her on the phone.

I jumped online and sent her an email in hopes that would reach her. I told her that I thought I needed to go to the hospital and that something was just not right. Something bad was going to happen and I was going to go through it alone.

I stood back up from my desk and due to the dizziness being so overwhelming, I fell directly to the floor. It was at that moment the phone rang.

I was moving so slowly, after about eight or nine rings, it stopped.

I literally crawled across the floor to the entertainment center the phone sat on. I pulled myself up and the phone started ringing again.

It was Christina. I explained to her the best I could what was going on, but my words were starting to slur and my vision was coming in and out of focus. She told me to hang up and immediately call 911.

Knowing my luck, I thought this would turn into the boy who cried wolf and no one would show up this time.

But I called anyway, and a dispatcher quickly answered.

She immediately asked what the emergency was and I explained to her all of my symptoms.

While I was talking to her my voice started to slur more and more as if I had been drinking large amounts of alcohol. I was standing there fearing the worst. I was fearing a stroke.

The dispatcher asked me a question and I answered silently in my head over and over before actually attempting to physically say it to her.

She said an ambulance was on the way. But I had another issue to tend to.

My dogs.

If the emergency responders came through my front door, they would be "what's for dinner."

I was so concerned I was going to pass out and they would be forced to enter the house and my dogs would go into protection mode. I paced and paced around the kitchen where I could see out into the driveway. With each step I took, I felt as if I was going to fall straight through the floor.

It was like that feeling when you are walking down a set of steps in the dark and you expect there to be one more step, but there isn't.

That's when I heard a little child laugh from another room. I stopped pacing immediately.

The dogs had stopped watching me and were now staring at our bedroom door.

Norman was laughing at me. There was no child in the house and there was nothing that could have made such a vivid and lifelike sound such as a little boy laughing.

My shock about the voice was interrupted when the phone rang again and since I was still gripping it in my hand, I answered it.

Christina was calling to tell me she was on the way and advised me to go outside and stay on the porch so the paramedics wouldn't have to bust our door down and become dog food.

She had caught up to an ambulance and there was a good chance it was the one heading directly for me.

The ambulance finally arrived and I did my best to make my way to the emergency vehicle. Two paramedics exited the vehicle and wasted no time attending to me. By this point my entire body was trembling and my heart was raising so fast. They placed me on a bed in the ambulance and started running tests.

The first test they did was an electrocardiogram (EKG). An EKG measures the electrical activity of your heart. Electrical activity is displayed as lines on paper, either spiking or dipping.

Mine was spiking so much it was nearly making a solid black mass across the paper.

My blood pressure was 220 over 140. That's the Grim Reaper standing beside you saying, "Hey, do you have plans for tonight?"

That meant this was a hypertensive crisis and a serious medical emergency. Blood pressure results that dangerously high typically end in a heart attack or stroke and death, so the paramedics prepared me for what they felt was inevitable.

Four baby aspirin were given to me along with intravenous fluids of this and that.

At this point I could barely speak and the body trembling had turned into full-blown convulsions.

Christina entered the ambulance, which was still parked in our yard, and filled in the paramedics on my medical history.

This may surprise you, but my medical history did not consist of anything heart or stroke related. I've never even broken a bone.

We finally pulled out of our driveway and flew like a bat out of hell to the hospital. Nothing had changed with my condition upon arrival.

Obviously, they needed to do more tests, but my body was not cooperating. I was shaking so much that Christina and a handful of nurses had to restrain my body just so they could take vial after vial of blood to run labs. After a slew of tests and medicines to stop the convulsing and bring my heart rate down, I was back to normal.

Within just a few hours I was ready to go home. The doctor came in and said he couldn't explain it. He would have bet on a heart attack any day; they were preparing for it.

They conducted a few final tests, did another EKG, and checked my blood pressure and everything came back perfect. And I mean perfect.

The doctor said someone couldn't ask for better blood tests results. I was in tip-top shape, or so they said. The doctor had no explanation as to why my body reacted the way it did that day. His response was, "We will call it a miracle."

Call it what you will, but I prefer to call it another stunt from the entity inside of Norman.

Shortly after I was discharged from the hospital, we returned home. The whole ordeal had left me so exhausted. I just hit the bed and found myself lost in thoughts about death.

I've spent a large portion of my life studying life after death, and in recent years I have come close to becoming death myself. I truly am blessed when it comes to that.

Years ago I flipped a car seven times and walked away with minor cuts, a body full of bruises, and post-traumatic stress disorder.

Even then, emergency responders expected the worst. They expected to find whoever was in the vehicle dead.

But I wasn't, and like this recent occurrence with my heart, the doctor who examined me after the crash said similar things.

He said, "Somebody must have been looking over you," or something like that. Considering my many scrimmages with death, I'm honestly surprised I don't have serious mental issues.

I guess that's subjective, considering I spend my time looking for ghosts.

I stared at the ceiling wondering what Norman's next move was going to be. I wondered why we were unable to rid ourselves of him, and I wondered just how far this was going to go.

He tried to murder me, but somehow, whether it be divine intervention, sheer luck, or just plain willpower, I survived another brush with death.

It would soon be Christmas Eve, and I don't think Norman really wanted me there—this was his way of trying to prevent that from being so.

But unless he made another effort to rid the house of a male presence, plans for Christmas were moving forward. Those plans involved filling the house with a lot of family—a lot of them being children and men.

I was hoping the symbolism behind all the 911 assumptions ended here. I was also wishing that the only thing lit up at the house would be festive lights and not a catastrophic and deadly fire.

15

Christmas Eve 2016

It was the night before Christmas and all through the house a creature was stirring...

It was Christmas Eve 2016. Festive lights flickered and danced over a blanket of North Carolina humidity.

People were rejoicing, singing, and enjoying laughs and the company of friends and family. There we stood...only we weren't the people rejoicing, singing, and enjoying laughs.

But it didn't start that way.

It had been years since Christina had the entire family over for Christmas. But it was important for her to do so. She was never really all that big on Christmas, but something was different with her this year. All of a sudden she had an almost questionable enthusiasm for the holly jolly holiday. Who was I to argue? I always enjoyed Christmas.

Believe it or not, it is my favorite month for movies. When I was younger, Christmas was it. I loved that time of year. The snow, the lights, and just the entire positive vibe.

So when Christina said she was going to hold a family Christmas at the house, I just couldn't say no. I was a bit skeptical considering the obvious worry of an explosion or fire or something terrible happening to one of us, or worse yet, one of the children. However, plans went forward regardless of a potential attack from Norman. History repeating itself had been a little too accurate up to this point, so you can imagine my concern.

And Christina's complete one-eighty from the anti-Christmas girl to the new spokesperson for the holiday kept my eyebrows raised.

Was this another Norman trick?

He can get into your head, and as I learned, he can squeeze the life out of you.

Whether I liked it or not, our house was going to be hosting the lights, magic stories, and carol of the bells for all the family to enjoy.

So as families do, we took the few days we had before Christmas and decorated. Our main focus was the living room, where the Christmas tree was placed. Lights were placed everywhere, as well as dozens of decorations throughout the house. The living room is where everybody would gather for the children to open their presents and for me to end up being a paranoid freak awaiting something demented from Norman. After all the tinsel, glow, and mistletoe, the house was ready.

Christmas Eve morning was a blur to me. It was as if I were half asleep and half awake most of the day. I felt like I was walking through our house and going through the motions, only the house was darker, different, and alive in some way.

You know when you dream and the perspective you tend to see during that time? That's what it felt like. It was like I was asleep and dreaming. I would hear Christina talk to me. I would hear the dogs barking. But everything sounded as if it were coming from the other side of a wall. It was muffled.

I don't know if it was nerves or full-on anxiety, but all morning long I felt as if I was going to have a massive panic attack.

It wasn't like before when I called for an ambulance. This was much different. I felt like I was in an alternate version of our house, yet everything was operating the same.

I needed to keep my mind occupied, so I decided to spend some time behind the computer and make a soundtrack full of Christmas songs to play during the gathering.

I mixed in everything from the classics to modern versions of them. I had a little something for everybody. From "Rudolph the Red-Nosed Reindeer" to the Trans-Siberian Orchestra performing holiday music.

Before anybody even arrived, I had the disc in the player out in the living room blasting the joyous melodies all day long. I was doing my best to keep the atmosphere as positive as possible.

Liam and Lyndsay were to be there and that of course rattled my nerves considering what happened with Norman during their last visit.

I'm still not certain what Norman's infatuation was with Liam and what Liam's infatuation was with Norman. But something was there. It was evident from the surveillance footage that Liam, although obsessed with the doll, held a little angst toward him too.

I hated to think the worst, but possession is a tricky phenomenon. I also hate to bring even more clichéd thoughts into this, but maybe Norman wanted to be Liam. Maybe Liam was to act as his new surrogate.

I don't know. At this point I wasn't going to give Norman the opportunity to do anything to harm the children. Invasion of the body snatchers wasn't exactly something I wished to ponder for too long.

I was going to keep him as far away from the children as possible. We all wanted this to be a joyous day.

Talking about or seeing a haunted doll that the entire family was now aware of certainly wasn't going to help bring out the Christmas spirit. No pun intended.

If all went as planned, our house would be hosting about twenty or more family guests.

I was hoping all of the positive energy from family would keep anything foreboding distant.

Norman was placed in the master bedroom where the children could not reach him or even think about him. He was out of sight.

Our situation this Christmas Eve was much different in comparison to the 1968 incident.

Those bearings involved a little girl, her mother, and of course Matty the doll.

Christmas Eve may have been a tragedy then, but the setup for us was contrasting and distant from that infamous night.

Everybody was to arrive at five-thirty that afternoon. Within minutes the house was full of conversation, laughs, presents, and kids running amok.

All the food that we prepared, coupled with what the others brought, placed an aroma in the house we all know too well around the holidays. Everybody was drinking and being merry, with the exception of me and a few others who wanted to keep a clear head. After dinner, everybody opened their gifts and the laughs and smiles continued. I too was starting to feel a little better about the night. All the same, my incessant need to observe every little detail in people from their vocal tone to their body movements still remained firmly in place.

That's when I started to notice a certain blanket of antagonism and dubiousness begin to overtake our company. Arguments were starting to break out between family members over the most trivial conditions. A few people left without saying a word, only to return more intoxicated than when they left. Red flags were popping up everywhere. Despite all of the colorful lights, the house was slowly becoming dark and gloomy.

As hosts tend to do at a party, I moved from group to group, being as entertaining as I possibly could.

I was just trying to lighten the mood.

Christina could tell something was off as well, so she too joined in on acting goofy and playing with the kids to keep the house upbeat. Still, the leeriness remained and I was reluctant to believe the source was something else. Christina's son Blake started acting very antisocial. It appeared as if every little thing was setting him off in a negative fashion.

All of the children became introverts all of a sudden. They were all sitting by themselves, either playing on a laptop, a cell phone, or some other portable gaming device.

The children would become angry if you approached them for any reason. For me, the room began to shrink. I was standing there trapped in tunnel vision.

However, with all of the distraction and my focus on the adults becoming more and more distant and agitated, I missed the fact that the music had reached the end of the disc I had playing.

Nobody even noticed the silence. They were all too preoccupied with their bickering and arguing.

At this point I was standing in the living room. I looked around wondering what the hell was going on to cause such a mood change in everybody.

Possession is typically a singular event. There was no way I was going to stand there believing everybody was individually becoming possessed. But they were being manipulated.

Possession and manipulation are two completely different actions. When one becomes possessed, they literally turn into a passenger inside their own body. Most possessions derive from malevolent entities controlling your body for evil purposes.

You become a remote-controlled vehicle. Your body is used to perform the task a spirit alone cannot. The same principle can be related to the haunting of dolls.

Manipulation, on the other hand, is a spirit affecting your environment with the goal of controlling it. I describe the difference like this: If you are exposed to the sun for long periods of time, you burn. The sun is now controlling your skin. If you stay inside, the sun heats up the house and you become hot and you sweat. The sun is now manipulating your environment. But all things, in the end, point to the sun.

Norman was changing our environment. The human body has an electrical component that reacts to other electrical components.

Norman was causing such negative energy within the house it was affecting all of us.

He just wanted to sit back and watch the show he was directing. Another perfect example of his sociopathic behavior.

You have heard people say, "I have a bad feeling about this," or "I get a bad feeling around him."

We do feel energy whether it is good or bad. I was starting to lose my mind. Everywhere I looked I saw Norman's face. The bodies of my family were the same, yet they all had his smiling face. It was frightening. The sounds in the room became more and more muffled. I felt like we were all crammed inside of an elevator with the oxygen running out.

The whole room had a haze to it. I was floating inside a mirage. Yet everything happening was real. I knew in my head that this illusion was either brought on from anxiety or Norman. Maybe both. But all adults accounted for were experiencing claustrophobia and the incessant need to go outside for air. So it wasn't just isolated to me.

Then something remarkable occurred, and nearly every one of us witnessed it.

I started focusing on Mason, Blake's son. He was watching cartoons on a tablet. He kept saying he wanted to watch *Frosty the Snowman*.

All my ears would fixate on was the fact he wanted *Frosty the Snowman*. That's all I heard over and over.

He eventually found it and the show started playing on his device.

Almost simultaneously, the DVD player started to operate again and the song "Frosty the Snowman" began to play.

I vividly remember Mason, myself, and Hannah promptly glancing over to the television.

My vision and hypnotic feelings all went back to normal at that moment. Hannah asked me if I had seen the DVD player start up on its own, and of course I had.

The really interesting part about the song playing by itself on the television was the fact it was far down the track list on the disc. So even if the DVD player had been set to repeat the disc, it would have never started with that song. Hannah and I grabbed Christina's attention and explained to her what had just happened.

She too was amazed and confused as to how that song could just randomly start playing through our television without human intervention.

Apparently, all Mason had to say was he wanted Frosty the Snowman and miraculously it was now playing off of the disc I created. The DVD player executes from start to finish. There was no *random* feature to explain that song popping up so we could all just call it coincidence.

That was no coincidence. It was paranormal.

I found myself in a trance, once again thinking back to the story of the girl standing in the snow as she watched her house burn to the ground.

Maybe it was the song that brought out that recollection. After our DVD player came to life, everybody was once again at each other's throats.

We had planned earlier to get couples pictures in front of the tree as well as pictures with the kids. So I brought it up while everybody was still there. Blake, who was the first to start acting off, told Christina he had to go, he couldn't take anymore. He said the anxiety was overwhelming.

So we quickly staged all of the planned pictures. After each couple had their picture taken, they left with kids in tow.

Within about fifteen minutes, the only people in the house were me, Christina, and Hannah.

I was relieved, in a way, that everybody was gone. I guess considering all things, bad attitudes and a song magically playing wasn't something to be all that concerned with.

The day had taken a lot out of us, though, between the cooking, the anxiety, and the entertaining, so Christina decided to retire for the night.

I stayed up and loaded all of the pictures into the computer to edit and share with the family within a day or so. I couldn't sleep anyway.

I just kept waiting for something electrical to go wrong or anything that would start a fire.

At about two in the morning I finally hit the bed. I still didn't sleep, though.

I just found myself lying in that same state I was getting used to, staring at the ceiling thinking about Norman.

My mind was racing with questions.

When are you going to do it? Where's the big finale? All this build up and for what? Are you finally done with the terrorizing?

I eventually fell asleep only to wake up in the middle of a panic attack with Christina by my side assuring me everything was alright.

I told her I could have sworn I opened my eyes and saw Norman standing on the floor by the bed, staring at me. That's when she paused and said, "Where is Norman?"

We both bounced out of bed to find him.

He was originally placed on top of our bookshelf, but now he wasn't there. My computer screen is always on, in addition to the surveillance monitor, so there was always enough light to see around the bedroom. Call it our nightlights, if you will. We panicked and turned on the bedroom light for better visibility.

He was gone.

How long he had been gone was the real question here. Ever since I had placed him on top of that shelf, I had not looked at him. I was wondering if somehow one of the kids managed to get him or if one of the adults was playing a prank. Unfortunately, that wasn't the case.

We woke Hannah up and conducted an extensive search of the house.

From under every bed to inside every dresser and cabinet, Norman was nowhere to be found.

I was even inspecting the dogs just in case they had decided to make him a chew toy.

To be honest, I was kind of hoping they had. Rationally speaking, I had no choice but to believe that somebody had taken him that evening. It wouldn't have been hard to do considering the amount of people and the amount of distraction.

But why?

To my knowledge those who witnessed firsthand his abilities wanted nothing to do with him. And those who heard the stories steered clear of him.

For now it was a mystery.

I stayed awake for the remainder of the night as did Hannah. She was so on edge that every little creak or click in the house caused her to jump and gasp or scream. I'm surprised Christina was even able to sleep.

Norman was missing. A burning question remained. Where was he?

Christmas morning came and there was Norman, sitting firmly where I had originally placed him the day before, on top of the book shelf.

I was beginning to think the events from the night prior were just a dream. I mean, I was really exhausted, so I was just going to keep my mouth shut until either Christina or Hannah brought it up.

If they didn't, I was chalking it up to a nightmare. Some things are just best left alone. But it didn't take long after they woke up for Hannah to come yelling at me. She thought it was me who pulled the prank and hid the doll.

She came into our bedroom and saw Norman where he was supposed to be. I assured her I had nothing to do with that doll being moved.

In her head, I think she was just trying to justify the horror we had been living since the summer.

Christmas came and went and we welcomed the New Year with hopes of less supernatural antagonizing and more solid conclusions on what to do with Norman. Somehow, 2017 was going to either close the chapter on our life with the doll or start a whole new one.

16

Ashes

Shortly after the New Year, Christina and I decided to revisit the old antique shop where we originally acquired Norman.

Believe it or not, even after over two months, the area was still struggling with the aftermath of Hurricane Matthew.

We live in the boondocks, so there are two speeds to just about everything here—slow and slower. But I honestly don't mind. In fact, that's why I love it here.

The hustle and bustle of the big cities just isn't for me. I gave New York City a shot once when I was younger. After college I gave a resort town a shot. So moving here was literally a breath of fresh air.

Piles of debris still layered the sides of just about every road we drove down that day.

Roads that had been washed out completely back in October were still large holes in the earth surrounded by detour signs.

During the drive, Christina and I were amazed at all of the still-visible damage. The drive back to the antique shop was farther than the drive we took just days after the hurricane initially hit. We were seeing destruction we never knew existed.

It was saddening to see homes completely destroyed. Large piles of furniture and the guts of houses lined up along the streets. Entire lives were erased in one night. It's scary when you think about how a single moment can change everything. What if we had never pulled Norman down off that shelf back in July 2016? What would our life be like at this moment?

That one decision altered our lives drastically for five months, and here we were heading back to the place he was discovered.

My main goal with this trip was to hopefully see the same ladies who sold him to us in the first place. Maybe there was more I could get out of them as far as the history of the doll.

As I neared the end of my book concerning our encounters and experiences with Norman, I couldn't help but attempt to find some sort of closure. Reality is reality, and when you write nonfiction, endings come by the will of reality.

We finally hit the long stretch of road that led to the shop. All that surrounded our drive for the next few miles was trees and swamp.

As we drew closer to the old shop, something seemed off. Out front were dozens of piles of debris and garbage. My first thought was that they suffered damage from the hurricane.

But that was shocking considering most businesses were back up and running and had been for months. We pulled into the driveway and drove very slowly around the piles of what we thought was trash. But it wasn't trash at all. We were staring at pile after pile of damaged and destroyed antiques.

Nearly the entire guts of this old antique shop had transformed into mountains of useless objects once full of history. History now in bits and pieces. Some of it actually looked salvageable. But apparently at this point there wasn't a care in the world for it.

Everything from inside the old store looked like a giant puzzle box dumped outside.

Old records, furniture, vintage signs, jewelry, tools, books, and everything in between sat there with a light-black glaze blanketing each mound.

Our Matty, our Norman, our puzzle we had to put together seemed more symbolic at that moment. The stories that went with every piece of ruined merchandise, the sentimental value that once was—it was all relative.

Our ending was to be found here. It was all gone and being prepared to be hauled off to a landfill. We pulled up to the front of the store and jumped out of the truck. Instantly, Christina and I were taken aback by the smell of soot and the remnants of fire. A smell I knew all too well growing up in a small coal-mining town in Western Maryland.

The doors to the shop were wide open, so we walked inside. To our surprise, the 4,200-square-foot store was nearly empty inside. The bones of the shop were charred and ash was everywhere. A handful of antiques remained, but they were one by one being carried out to the piles by various volunteers.

We continued to walk through the rubble when we heard a familiar voice. "The box is gone too, young man."

I turned to look and it was the woman who sold us Norman. I was completely shocked she remembered us. I wasn't sure if that was a good or bad thing.

Of course, she followed that up by telling us there wasn't much to see here now, and she was sorry the box was lost. I told her I didn't care about the box. I was more curious as to what happened.

I asked her if this was a result of Hurricane Matthew, even though deep down I knew there was no way that much time had passed and they were just now cleaning up.

The lady sighed and said they believed a fire was started by an electrical malfunction of some sort. Nobody knew for sure.

She also mumbled and griped about her husband Ed, who was always smoking in the store. The shop sat in such a remote place that nobody would have even seen it burning.

As far as the main structure, it was saved for the most part due to the sprinkler system. As ghastly as they looked, the bones of the shop remained, but the soul was gone. I could tell the lady really didn't want to talk for too long. I think she was ready to get the cleaning up over with and move on.

She said they had been at it for a week already. As we started to give our condolences and say goodbye, she thanked us for once again stopping by. I asked if the store would ever reopen.

She said it took so long for them to start the business and acquire everything. The store was their entire life. She added that it was her belief that what happened was a sign from God and it was time for them to move on. She was exhausted and ready to close that chapter of her life.

The last thing she said was "The place looks like hell now anyway...nobody wants to be here."

As we walked away I turned back around and said, "Something coming from hell was bound to look like it."

Christina and I left, jumped in the truck, and headed home. I told her that was it, that was the end, that was the fire. Everything came full circle. From beginning to end to another beginning with another ending. Christina was surprised I never inquired about when the fire actually took place.

I told Christina I didn't have to, the old woman already told us. I had the end of my book. Whether or not it was going to be the end of Norman was a different story.

But we could at least put him to rest.

Rest

After consulting other researchers educated and experienced with this sort of phenomena, coupled with our own professional data and opinions, Christina and I decided to lay Norman to rest.

We considered many options, including burning him, but that felt so heartless.

You may be sitting there wondering how anybody could have compassion for such an evil thing, but he was once human and that is something we are constantly reminded of.

I had thought maybe all Norman ever wanted was a proper burial. If he was indeed the spirit of that unborn boy from over five decades ago and he was trapped inside this plastic toy, well, maybe all he wanted was a normal end to it all. I considered finding a metal trunk with locks as his casket and putting him in the ground in the yard.

But what if we ever moved? What if one of the dogs dug him up?

It was all too risky to leave his fate, or somebody else's, to chance.

But with all of that under consideration, I still needed to keep my views rooted in a humanistic fashion. Would I burn a baby? Would I burn an old man?

No, I would not.

He was once human, so he needed to be treated as such, whether I agreed with his actions or not. Maybe that's all he wanted. Maybe all he ever wanted was to be treated like a little boy, have his own room and toys, and live the life that was never given to him.

Too often morals and ethics are tossed aside and forgotten about in the field of paranormal research. Too often the spirits are treated like a sideshow act versus the human that once was.

Christina agreed since at this point it was certainly not going to hurt to try. I mean, nothing else had worked, so what did we have to lose? We needed to give Norman what he possibly wanted but also keep him contained, away from others and placed in a controlled environment to keep our family safe. So we gave Norman his own room, but with a catch.

We had a spare room that was being used for storage. There was already a bed in there and two dressers. It really was just a junk room. We relocated most of the junk and things none of us used anymore, and we started turning it into a room for a little boy.

Toys, games, and even a television were all brought in. We left the television on a cartoon station. There was one window in the room and we sealed that from the outside with plywood and siding. The area quickly became isolated from the outside world.

Our junk room had been transformed into a room fit for a little boy in the course of a day.

At first we thought we would try that option to see if the activity ceased and Norman found his peace. If not, we planned to make the necessary changes to suit an old man, because we still needed to remember he could possibly have mentally grown to be what would be a fifty-four-year-old man. However, our initial experiment proved to be a success.

Once Norman was placed in the newly renovated children's room, all activity in our house went flat. We had our seminormal life back.

But there was a catch. Norman's room was sealed and locked from the outside. Only we had possession of the key. We placed a sign on the door that said Authorized Personnel Only, which we acquired from another antique shop.

Please pardon our so-so painting job. We were still in recovery from household damages caused by the hurricane and Norman.

Seventeen

The door to Norman's room.

As a precaution, just in case anything ever happened to us and somebody had to enter without knowledge of what was behind the door, we placed an unbelievable list of instructions and accounts with Norman in an envelope below the doorknob.

The envelope read, "If you must enter, please read. Hell awaits."

I'm sure any sane individual would read that and laugh it off. But that was the best we could do.

I also wired up a few surveillance cameras to monitor anybody or anything that approached the door.

I left the interior alone.

That was Norman's room now and it seemed to keep him happy and away from harming us.

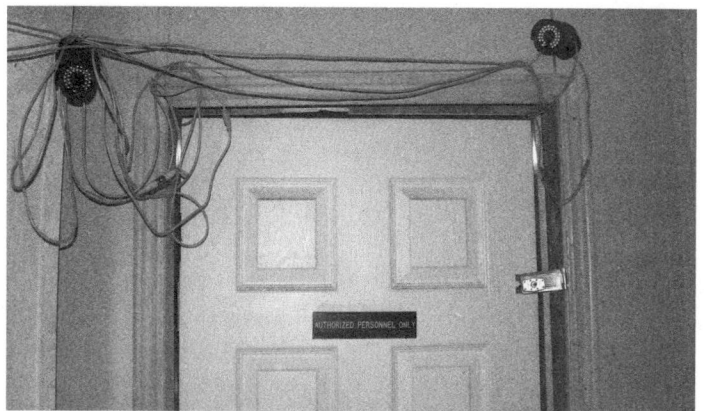
Twenty-four hour surveillance monitors his door.

Believe me when I tell you that door has been a conversation piece with every guest we welcome into our home. The conversation typically leads to us showing our guests the surveillance footage, and we get to witness our friends and family dropping their jaws in awe.

Occasionally I will walk up to the door just to listen, and once in a while I will hear the sound of the television.

It's quite spooky, frankly, because each and every time I do that, the television stops as if he knows I'm right outside the door.

So I quietly walk away and leave him alone. Other nights we will be in our beds retiring for the evening and hear light knocks coming from his wall.

His sounds have become a part of the house speaking when it's quiet.

Occasionally we will hear the creak of an old rocking chair we placed in the room. Other times, we will hear a child laughing.

Easily dismissed, as most of the sounds can be considered the television. It's when you hear those sounds with the television off that it becomes haunting.

You quickly realize that the television cannot possibly be turning itself off and on, and you quickly accept the other sounds as Norman.

As evil as Norman is, he now has his childhood back—at least to a degree. As long as he is happy, we are happy. People are safe.

I still occasionally wake up with visions of him on top of me with a knife to my throat or standing by the bed watching. I still lie awake at night imagining his little feet tapping the floor as he is running through the house.

I guess you could say my family and I suffer from post-traumatic stress disorder because of the events that took place in our home. As I sit here at my desk, next to the bed, I can't help but glance across the headboard that showcases all of the other allegedly haunted dolls and toys we have acquired.

That alone gives me an uneasy feeling.

What if?

I will never look at toys and dolls the same way again. It is difficult for me to sleep soundly at night, knowing all of these toys are around me, considering what took place with Norman.

I'm not sure what the future holds for us or Norman. But we had to make a choice between living with him or in fear of him.

Afterword

Why not run? Why not flee the home?

Aren't those the very questions you ask yourself when reading about a haunting or watching a horror movie?

Maybe you question why it is not being destroyed? But can you really destroy a spirit? Maybe the shell he resides in, but the spiritual energy?

I don't think so.

On top of that, I am a paranormal researcher. I have spent twenty years seeking out supernatural phenomena. You have to take the good with the bad. No science lesson is learned without trial and error.

That's why we didn't run. That's why we didn't burn his plastic and cloth body. This is our job, whether it be for a client or personal work for ourselves.

We would have been fools to pass this opportunity up, even considering how outrageous and dangerous it ended up being. I know many of you readers are going to want to see the surveillance footage described in this book, and I don't blame you. After reading about all of the amazing occurrences, I too would be champing at the bit to see the real deal.

At the moment, I'm not sure what we are going to do with it. That would be a big step for us.

I know it sounds like a cop-out—an excuse to exaggerate actual events—but what would you do? Would you allow millions of people into your life and home?

If we release the surveillance clips for all the world to see, we release our private life.

Our bedrooms, our animals, our lifestyle, all of our possessions would become common knowledge, and that's a big risk to take.

If it were a commercial location, or even personal property with the proper permissions, we would release it in a heartbeat. But this is our home and our life and our story.

The last thing we want is for our lives to be invaded and our home to become a haunted stop for selfies and pictures in front of the "Norman House."

However, the other side of me wants you to see what we saw. I want you to feel that fear and consider all that happened because you saw it for yourself.

Time will tell.

Maybe if and when we move, the footage will become publicly accessible. If it does, it will show up on my respective social networking sites listed at the beginning of this book. For now, it's under lock and key, just like the subject at hand. I can tell you this: a handful of researchers have seen it.

The wonderful and highly respected Rosemary Ellen Guiley, who provided the foreword for this book, and the innovator himself, Darren Evans, who provided the epilogue, have reviewed all of the evidence, just to name a few.

Our close family members have not only seen it but have had their own experiences with the doll—experiences that were left out of this book, per request.

Only you can decide how you walk away from this ghost story.

You will either believe it or you won't.

If you had asked me five, ten, or even twenty years ago if I subscribed to the idea of haunted dolls, I would have laughed and given a stern no. But things change. Life has a way of doing that.

Norman has caused me to question my own beliefs and my own spirituality. Some things are just beyond what we can comprehend.

You would be surprised at the subculture that exists: an underground circuit using truth as science instead of science determining truth.

Afterword

I thank you, my friends, for once again reading about my work in the field of paranormal research. Whatever your motive or purpose for showing such an interest in my stories, you are truly appreciated. If you have followed along with my chronicles, you have probably noticed how my views on things have changed since the beginning.

Paranormal research is always changing, from the level of activity to the results of the investigative work. The possibilities are endless.

I have witnessed a lot and I couldn't be more blessed to still be alive to share my experiences. This was also new ground to break for me. Norman was a story that deserved its own in full.

Maybe there will be more from Norman. Maybe there won't. Maybe he will move on to wherever it is he needs to be, or maybe he will remain under our lock and key.

We are all haunted by something. Even those behind this curious activity are haunted in their own way. Maybe they are haunted by us.

We all have ghosts and monsters under the bed and skeletons in the closet, but so do they, them, and those. We tend to look at paranormal research as a two-way mirror where the afterlife can look in, only we can't look out. I often wonder what it is like to see the life you once lived and to see those friends and loved ones you once knew, yet they can't see you. Is it damnation or a blessing?

Where one may view the constant reminder of a life once lived as a curse, another may view it as a blessing that means nothing ever truly dies—good or bad.

There will always be a window to look out, or in, depending on which side you are on.

You will hear from me again...probably when we need a babysitter.

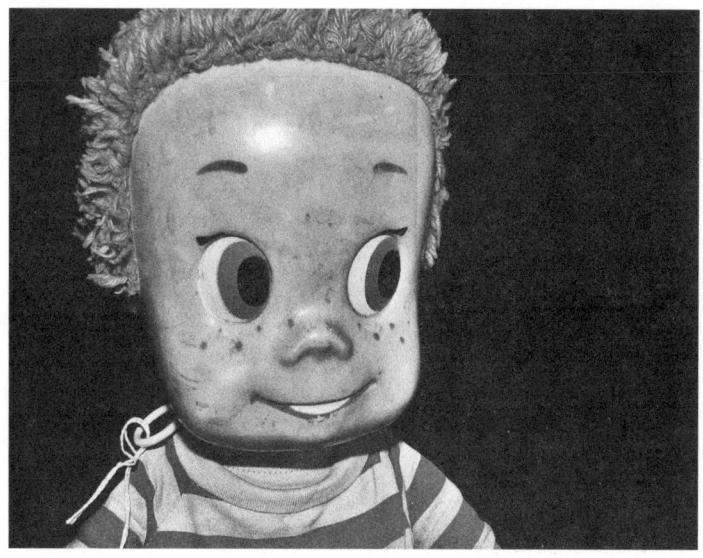

Norman, 2016.

Epilogue

Norman...think about it. The name Norman...you ever known anyone to answer by it? Me neither. But it's a name that is rooted in horror.

Hitchcock's psychopathic drama has painted shower curtains for half a century. A "slasher" was born.

My research into what has become known as the ZoZo Phenomenon is rooted in a sort of paranormal etymology. Basically a system of ever-changing name recognition.

Ancients believed certain names held powers. These perspectives continue into our modern beliefs that are actually based on centuries of mythology and fairy tales. But what happens when you see something you cannot believe?

Most people can probably do without seeing a creepy ventriloquist-looking doll subtlety moving at will. Thanks to Stephen Lancaster, it matters not my probability. Time and time again I see what my eyes should not.

Most of us would never find ourselves in a scene of child's play involving the name Chucky, where souls of the dead invade lifeless toys. In countless ghost stories, both in film and around campfires, dark spirits infiltrate toy rooms and dolls.

The problem is... many of these stories exist in our own homes.

I'm looking forward to hearing more of this Norman. As long as it's in someone else's Motel!

—Darren Evans

Darren Evans is a paranormal investigator, researcher, and a "paranormal survivor" of years of problems with ZoZo, starting with his board activity in 1982. Evans has been featured on television programs, including one of the highest-ever-rated episodes of "Ghost Adventures." He has played himself in films, and is a frequent guest on radio shows. Evans pioneered the research on "The ZoZo Phenomenon," revealing it to be worldwide.

GET MORE AT LLEWELLYN.COM

Visit us online to browse hundreds of our books and decks, plus sign up to receive our e-newsletters and exclusive online offers.

- Free tarot readings • Spell-a-Day • Moon phases
- Recipes, spells, and tips • Blogs • Encyclopedia
- Author interviews, articles, and upcoming events

GET SOCIAL WITH LLEWELLYN

Find us on **f**
www.Facebook.com/LlewellynBooks

 @LlewellynBooks

GET BOOKS AT LLEWELLYN

LLEWELLYN ORDERING INFORMATION

Order online: Visit our website at www.llewellyn.com to select your books and place an order on our secure server.

Order by phone:
- Call toll free within the US at 1-877-NEW-WRLD (1-877-639-9753)
- We accept VISA, MasterCard, American Express, and Discover.
- Canadian customers must use credit cards.

Order by mail:
Send the full price of your order (MN residents add 6.875% sales tax) in US funds plus postage and handling to: Llewellyn Worldwide, 2143 Woodale Drive, Woodbury, MN 55125-2989

POSTAGE AND HANDLING

STANDARD (US):
(Please allow 12 business days)
$30.00 and under, add $6.00.
$30.01 and over, FREE SHIPPING.

INTERNATIONAL ORDERS,
INCLUDING CANADA:
$16.00 for one book, plus $3.00 for each additional book.

Visit us online for more shipping options.
Prices subject to change.

FREE CATALOG!

To order, call
1-877-NEW-WRLD
ext. 8236
or visit our website